JOHN REDMAN'S
ESSENTIALS
OF THE
Golf Swing

JOHN REDMAN'S ESSENTIALS

OF THE

Golf Swing

by
JOHN REDMAN

and
Michael E. Thomason

A DUTTON BOOK

DUTTON
Published by the Penguin Group
Penguin Books USA Inc., 375 Hudson Street,
New York, New York 10014, U.S.A.
Penguin Books Ltd, 27 Wrights Lane,
London W8 5TZ, England
Penguin Books Australia Ltd, Ringwood,
Victoria, Australia
Penguin Books Canada Ltd, 10 Alcorn Avenue,
Toronto, Ontario, Canada M4V 3B2
Penguin Books (N.Z.) Ltd, 182–190 Wairau Road,
Auckland 10, New Zealand

Penguin Books Ltd, Registered Offices:
Harmondsworth, Middlesex, England

First published by Dutton, an imprint of New American Library,
a division of Penguin Books USA Inc.
Distributed in Canada by McClelland & Stewart Inc.

First Printing, May, 1993
10 9 8 7 6 5 4 3 2 1

 REGISTERED TRADEMARK—MARCA REGISTRADA

LIBRARY OF CONGRESS CATALOGING IN PUBLICATION DATA:
Redman, John (Rankin, John)
    [Essentials of the golf swing]
    John Redman's essentials of the golf swing/by John Redman and Michael E.
Thomason.
        p.   cm.
    Includes bibliographical references (p.).
    ISBN 0-525-93603-3
    1. Swing (Golf)   I. Thomason, Michael E.   II. Title.   III. Title: Essentials of the
golf swing.
GV979.S9R43   1992
796.352′3—dc20   92—36437
                                                              CIP

Printed in the United States of America
Set in Aster, Univers
Designed by Dorothy L. Gordineer/Libra Graphics

To all of my teachers and all of my students.
J.R.

To Lezette.
M.T.

To our editor Kevin Mulroy and his staff at NAL/Dutton, to our agent Elizabeth Kaplan, to our photographers Joseph Jenks of North Palm Beach, Steve Spatafore of Las Vegas, and Lauren Wilder of Las Vegas, and to our friend Paul Azinger,

Thank you.

CONTENTS

FOREWORD

by Paul Azinger

I first met John Redman during my freshman year at college. He was operating a driving range then and I went to see him on the recommendation of my college golf coach. At the time, I was just an average golfer. I'd never broken 70 and seldom broke 80 two days in a row. Three years later, with John's considerable help, I was on the PGA Tour, competing against the world's best.

Sure, I had some God-given talent and I practiced hard, hitting hundreds of balls every day, but John gave me excellent instruction. He recognized that my swing was too long and "flippy" at the top. So the first thing we worked on was shortening my swing. Then he taught me how to use my legs and hips and how to turn level both back and through. As you'll soon find out, that's a big part of his teaching. He also taught me to keep my hands and arms relaxed and to feel the weight of the club head on the end of the shaft.

John made a lot of changes to my swing, but the one thing he didn't change was my grip. I play with what many people call a strong grip. With most teachers, it wouldn't have lasted long. But, fortunately, John had the insight not to change it. He said that grip was natural for me and that's how he wanted me to hold the club.

Today, I look back and see how nicely my grip worked into John's teaching. My swing is just a level turn to the right, then a level turn back through the hitting area with my hands and arms relaxed. As a result, I go through impact "knuckles up" with the back of my left hand facing the sky, holding the attack angle longer than most players. It's a simple, accurate, and powerful way to hit the ball. I'm never "hands" conscious and seldom hook a shot. That's ironic because a lot of golfers I see with weak grips often hook the ball by over-rotating their hands, trying not to block it. As a matter of fact, I became a consistent money winner after John taught me how to fade the ball and still have the club head release fully. My grip, which many would have considered a liability, has turned out to be one of my biggest assets. But that's John for you.

I'm very glad he's written this book. Traveling as I do and playing in pro-ams every week, I've seen so many golfers who could benefit from John's natural, non-technical swing. He's been accessible to tour players for years and to list the ones he's worked with would take several pages. But amateurs wanting his help had to schedule lessons in advance, then travel to Orlando or Las Vegas. Now, all you have to do is get in your car and drive to the local bookstore.

It's one thing to take an excellent golfer, make some adjustment to his stance, his ball position, or some such, and marginally improve his play for a few weeks. There are a lot of teachers who can do that. There aren't many, however, who can take someone as mediocre as I was and in three years have him playing the Tour. But that's exactly what John Redman did.

I think that speaks for itself.

INTRODUCTION

In the memory of every golfer is a collection of "perfect" shots, like shiny trophies on a shelf somewhere in the back of his mind. Maybe, in your case, it includes a drive, one that split the fairway on the eighteenth hole, twenty yards farther than you'd ever hit it before. Later, you could still feel that pleasurable tingle in your hands when you replayed it mentally.

Perhaps there's a bullet of a long iron in the collection, too, one that started low, climbed high, then descended softly to the green, leaving your Saturday-morning cronies stunned and you with a ten-footer for birdie. Or maybe a wedge that seemed to leap from the club face, soaring like a bird before it fell out of the blue sky, stiff on the flag.

You knew instantly that was the way it was supposed to feel, the way you wanted to hit every shot. But when you tried to repeat it, you couldn't. Why? Because you didn't know how you had done it. I can only guess at all the sensations you experienced when hitting those shots, but I'd be willing to bet those swings felt powerful yet uninhibited; all the pieces seemed to fall into place and everything flowed toward the target.

Most people hit more of those perfect shots on the driving

range when they're under no pressure to produce, when they're taking practice swings and the ball just seems to get in the way of the club. But on the course it's a different story.

They step up to the ball and the cold fingers of "hit anxiety" grab them by the throats. Their hands tighten on the grip, tension wicks up their arms like creeping poison, and in seconds, that relaxed, driving-range swing with all its silky sensations is gone. The result is usually some tight, labored lunge, producing a smothered hook or a banana slice that wings over like a stunt plane at an air show. And if by some chance the ball does go straight, it usually flies about as far as a sick canary.

Golf can be a tough game. To generate power, you must stand to the side, unable to face the target the way you can with other sports. It's a position your eyes and brain don't like. Then your first move isn't to turn toward your target, but to turn away from it! And all the while, a little voice in your head is saying, "No, no. There's no way this ball is going where you want it to go." Things can really get dicey when there's something like a lake to your left or out of bounds right. So, on the way down, you're overcome by this impulse to "help" things in some way (usually with your hands), and you end up ruining the shot.

If I've heard it once, I've heard it a thousand times: "Why can't I just relax and hit it with a practice swing?"

Well, I have some good news. I can explain how you hit those perfect shots, and more important, I can show you how to hit them again and again.

I can teach you how to hit it with your practice swing.

For forty years, I've been searching for a better way to swing the club. Nothing unusual about that—every golfer who's ever lived has been on the same mission. But I've been blessed with certain advantages. You might say my research library is better than most.

In the early 1950s, while I was in the service and stationed in Japan, Tommy Armour's *How to Play Your Best Golf All the Time* was my constant companion. Then, several years later, I had the incredibly good fortune of meeting him and becoming his student and friend. How many people have the opportunity to become friends with their heroes?

I studied with him, listened to his every word, and watched him give hundreds of lessons. I took a few myself. And, of course, we played a lot of golf together. His memory still casts a long shadow in my life.

It was from Mr. Armour that I learned that the art of demonstration is one of the best tools a teaching professional can have. For instance, if he saw something he didn't like, he'd get off his stool and show you what he wanted. To this day, I don't ask my students to do anything I can't do myself, and that goes for everything in this book.

I worked for Sam Snead, another hero, and teed it up with him more times than I can remember. Sam may be the finest athlete who's ever played the game; just watching him swing was a clinic. I've played many rounds with Julius Boros in south Florida. Big Julius had the laziest, most beautiful tempo of anybody I've ever seen. He held the club lightly, made a nice turn, and then went through the ball as if he were cutting a piece of cake.

I've given countless lessons, and I've never given a lesson during which I didn't receive one in return. The golf books and magazines I've read would easily fill a room. I've played in many competitions with players I thought had good swings, and I've always paid particular attention to the swings that produced the really good-sounding shots and the correct trajectories.

I noticed other things, too. For instance, I've never seen a good player with a weak grip or a wide stance. I've never seen a good player who didn't take an athletic stance. I've never stood behind a good player and not been able to see his left knee at address. I've never seen a good player who didn't turn his left shoulder "up" to his chin on his backswing. I've never seen a good player who took the club straight back for any distance. I've never seen a good player who picked the club up abruptly on the backswing. I've never seen a good player with a full turn who didn't cross the line at the top. I've never seen a good player who started down by pulling his hands toward the ball. I've never seen a good player who hit the ball off his right foot. I've never seen a good player whose hips weren't turned out of the way and whose weight wasn't on his left side at impact. I've never seen a good player who kept his head perfectly still or his left arm perfectly straight. I've never seen a good player with a weak little finger on his left hand. I've never seen a good player who wasn't fighting a hook, and I've never seen a good player who could satisfactorily explain what he was doing. After more than thirty-five years as a teaching professional, I've noticed many things.

I've also had the pleasure of working with a number of fine young men and women on the PGA and LPGA tours. They're talented, hardworking, and dedicated, and I live and die vicariously with their triumphs and defeats.

A very special student is Paul Azinger, who came to me in 1979 as a promising but inconsistent junior college golfer. Today he's one of the finest golfers in the world, and I'm very proud of what he's accomplished. Although he was named PGA Tour Player of the Year in 1987 and is at or near the top of the money list season after season, it's apparent from their remarks that most golf commentators don't fully understand what we've accomplished with his "strong" grip (their choice of words, not mine).

Remember I said I was searching for a better way of swinging the golf club? Well, I've found it and Paul uses it. If the PGA Tour is a gunfight, Paul's packing a better pistol.

What I teach is a swing that is powerful, accurate, and repeatable, as well as being simple and natural. Its advantages are many, and here are a few:

1. It has fewer moving parts, so to speak, so it's more dependable, especially under pressure.

2. It employs only natural positions and movements, so you're not building up a lot of stress on the backswing—stress that can result in "hitting from the top."

3. It's a swing that works *with* the body, not *against* it, so you won't be making appointments with the chiropractor or wearing bandages for tendinitis.

4. It features a "natural" grip and wrist cock that allows you to swing the club on a more upright plane. That means the club face will remain square to the target longer in the hitting area, increasing the chances of an accurate shot.

5. It's a pure centrifugal-force swing with no lateral movement, producing a very true action at impact for accuracy. It's also easy to repeat.

6. And it will generate the greatest amount of clubhead speed that a particular golfer's physique is capable of generating. I'm not saying you'll hit the ball as far as the Zinger does, but you'll hit it as far as you're capable of hitting it.

In short, with this swing you'll be able to play to your full potential. I know that's promising a lot, but I'm confident I can deliver.

However, there is one warning. If you're a buttoned-down conformist, you may want to look elsewhere for assistance. Peer pressure can be intense, and much of what I teach challenges "modern" theory. If playing one of the currently fashionable "designer" swings (as a student of mine calls them) is more important to you than the numbers on your scorecard, then this book is not for you. But if you're an individualist and you want to improve your game, then I can help.

I've been told that what I teach is unique. Maybe the synthesis of ideas is, but every fundamental presented here can be found elsewhere in the rich and abundant literature of the game. In the first chapter of Ecclesiastes, a very wise man wrote that, "there is nothing new under the sun." If I didn't know better, I would think he was referring to methods of striking a golf ball. People have been scribbling fervently about this game since before Bonnie Prince Charlie was hacking it out of the heather in Scotland 250 years ago, and they've produced a lot of books.

So why am I writing another?

Because I believe that for the vast majority of players, the swing I teach is better than anything else that's being taught today. Since the late 1950s, there's been a constant parade of new swing theories and techniques, and while I'm sure that they were well-intentioned, I find most of them contrived, artificial, and unnecessarily complicated.

By the way, though my swing is "better," it is not "new." It's a classic, and the years have done nothing to make it less effective. It's basically the swing that Tommy Armour and Percy Boomer taught, with a few improvements of my own.

After a discussion of centrifugal force, there are only four fundamentals—grip, stance, takeaway, and position of the club at the top. I'll present them to you with simple words and easy-to-grasp concepts. So, if you're ready to post lower scores, let me show you how to turn and hit it with your practice swing!

John Redman's
Essentials
OF THE
Golf Swing

CENTRIFUGAL FORCE

When working with a new student, I always begin the first lesson with this demonstration. Holding the grip of a club between my left thumb and index finger, I lift the shaft with my right hand and let it go. This sets the club swinging back and forth like the pendulum of a grandfather clock. I tell every student that because I'm holding it lightly, the club will swing by itself until gravity and friction eventually stop it.

There are other things I point out about my golf-club pendulum—the vertical plane in which it swings; how it retraces its path or arc each time because it's swinging from a fixed point; its easy but purposeful pace; and how it seems to pause as it changes directions, as if gathering itself for the return trip.

The second part of my demonstration concerns adding power, because I wouldn't be able to hit the ball very far with just the momentum of the pendulum. Adding power is simple. I turn my hips first to the right, leading the swinging club in that direction, then turn them back to the left, and the club follows, swinging farther and faster. Actually, I'm pulling the club with the motion of my hips. If you haven't done so already, I would encourage you to get a club and try it for yourself. (If you're hav-

The club should swing like a pendulum.

ing trouble with tempo while playing, swinging the club like a pendulum as you walk down the fairway will help.)

In a sense, this is the golf swing I teach in its simplest form. I turn my hips to the right on a level plane and the club swings back and up. Then I turn my hips to the left, again on a level plane, and the club swings down and through. The lower body acts, the upper body reacts. You could think of it as just two turns and two "lags"—a hip turn followed by a lagging club head, then another hip turn again followed by a lagging club head.

There's another demonstration I like to use, and since most people can find a piece of string and a metal washer (or some other small, weighted object) in that kitchen junk drawer, it's

To add power, turn your hips.

The washer will spin faster and its orbit will remain truer the steadier I keep my hand.

However, when I move my hand around, the washer slows and its orbit becomes erratic.

easy to perform, too. Just tie one end of the string to the washer, hold the other end, and spin the washer around your hand. Again, there are things to notice and lessons to be learned.

See how the washer spins faster and its orbit stays truer the steadier you keep your hand. But move your hand around, shifting it from side to side, for example, and notice how the washer slows down and its path becomes erratic. Move your hand enough and the washer will even fall out of its orbit.

The path of the washer can be affected by something else, as well. What if the string twists and a kink or knot develops? Obviously, the radius (the length of string measured from your hand to the washer) will be shortened, and the washer's speed will be disrupted until it settles into another orbit.

Let's compare this to the golf swing. Imagine that the washer is the head of your club, the hand holding the string is your body, and the piece of string linking the two is your arms, your hands, and the club shaft. You turn your body, just as you spin the string with your hand, to make your linkage (i.e., arms, hands, and club shaft) move. And because the club head is connected to your linkage, it also moves. You are actually swinging the club head with your lower body, or more specifically, as I teach it, with your hips.

I mentioned above that the orbit and speed of the spinning washer would be affected if you moved your hand about or allowed a knot or kink to develop in the string. Are there analogous things that influence the golf swing, as well?

For instance, what if you moved your body laterally as you swung, deliberately trying to shift your weight from one foot to the other? Would that have an effect on the speed or path of the club head? What if you gripped the club tightly or tried to manipulate it by rolling your forearms over as you hit the ball? Would that have any effect?

Of course. Any of those things can affect the quality of the shot, and usually for the worse. In my opinion, they're unnecessary and often harmful complications. That's why I don't teach them. However, as you might have guessed, they do have their proponents.

The term commonly used to refer to this circular, swinging-around-a-fixed-point type of motion is centrifugal force. Technically, that's inaccurate, because centrifugal force is actually the name for the *outward pull* you feel when you spin the washer and create this rotary or curvilinear motion. I'll use the term loosely, however, like others who have written about the golf swing before me, because strict scientific usage serves no purpose here.

A swing based on centrifugal force offers substantial benefits. First, it's a powerful swing. Distance is a function of club-head speed squarely applied. The faster you can make the club head move, the farther you can hit the ball, and you can move the club head faster by swinging it than by any other way.

Consider the confrontation between David, with his sling, and Goliath. For those of you who came in late, a sling is a primitive weapon used for throwing stones. It consists of a piece of leather tied to cords that are whirled by hand. Now, a sling and a golf club aren't exactly the same, but they share two important characteristics—both are used to launch missiles and both perform most powerfully when swung. With his sling, David threw a stone with such force that it killed a giant. There are many skilled golfers who, with a club and ball, could literally accomplish the same thing.

A centrifugal-force swing is accurate and repeatable. Think about the washer tied to the end of a string. With every revolution, the washer retraces the same orbit. The club head does much the same thing, returning to its "square" address position at impact, swing after swing after swing.

A centrifugal-force swing is also simple to understand because everyday examples are all around us: the farm boy who swings the pail of milk over his head without spilling a drop, the earth orbiting the sun, satellites orbiting the earth, an athlete throwing the discus at a track and field meet.

Perhaps the most famous demonstration of centrifugal force in the golf swing was made by Ernest Jones with a jackknife and a handkerchief. Jones, an Englishman, lost a leg in World War I. He had been a scratch player before the war and, much to everyone's surprise, returned to shoot par golf again after the war, on one leg! Later, he became a celebrated instructor, and in several books he attributed his good play to "swinging the club head," which was how he described the use of centrifugal force in striking the ball. He said that the greatest obstacle to swinging correctly was the use of "leverage." By that, Jones meant applying pressure to the *side* of the shaft with the hands to make the club head move.

To demonstrate the correct way to swing the club head, he tied his jackknife to the end of a handkerchief and swung it. Because the handkerchief was flexible, he couldn't use it as a lever and therefore couldn't set the jackknife in motion by applying pressure to it.

He recommended the following drill to anyone who wanted

to learn how to swing properly. First, tie a small weight to one end of a string, just as I did for the washer-and-string demonstration above. Then grip both a golf club and the other end of the string in one hand and try to swing them together. If you use leverage—that is, pushing or pulling on the *side* of the shaft—the club head will move but the weight won't. Only by swinging the club correctly can you make the weight swing, too.

To convey the same idea, I often tell students to imagine they're swinging a rope with a rock tied to the end. That's what Charles Lamb, a Scottish professional, told me when I was a boy, caddying at the local club back home in Henderson, Kentucky. It's great advice to help cure "hitting from the top," a common result of trying to use the club like a lever. It's also an excellent way to restore lost tempo.

Now, what does all of this have to do with hitting it with your practice swing?

Quite a lot, actually. Think of what happens when you take a practice swing. First, your body turns freely because you're relaxed. Second, your grip is light because you're not trying to hit a ball. As a result, you often hear the club make a "whoosh" sound through the bottom part of the downswing arc. That's the sound of club-head speed, by the way.

Something similar happens from time to time when you're hitting lay-up shots. Does this sound familiar? You're playing a par-5 hole with a lake in front of the green, or maybe it's a sand trap you want to avoid. Because you can't reach the green in two shots, you select a short club to lay up with and take an easy swing. What happens? The ball leaves like a streak, sails farther than you ever thought possible, and splashes into the lake after a hop or two. Aaaah, the perfect shot and what a time to hit it!

That was *your practice swing with a ball in the way*. Consider it a lucky accident, even if it did ruin your score on that hole, because it was just what we're looking for. How did it happen? You were relaxed because you weren't trying to hit the ball hard, so you held the club lightly and turned your body freely. As I said, you made your practice swing with a ball in the way.

**Swinging a practice club with a very flexible shaft is
similar to swinging a rope with a rock tied to one end.**

Think back to the washer-and-string demonstration and remember how I compared it to the golf swing. The washer was
the club head, the string was your hands and arms, and the hand
that held the string was your body. See the similarities? *You
swing the club head with your freely turning body* while *your
hands and arms serve only as a passive link.*

Now, contrast that to the normal swing of a typical high-
handicapper. He addresses the ball feeling anxious, wanting to
get it over with as quickly as possible. There's tension in his

hands and forearms, which causes him to squeeze the grip tightly. He probably has very little awareness of his lower body, a consequence of upper-body tension, and his legs and hips might as well be wooden for all the sensory information his brain is receiving from them. As a result, his normal swing is an abrupt hands-and-arms effort that usually leaves him off balance and falling backward.

When taking a practice swing, you hold the club lightly and turn your body freely because you're relaxed. But when actually hitting a shot (if you're like a lot of golfers), you tense up and squeeze the club, restricting your body's ability to turn. If you have a tight grip, there's little prospect of centrifugal force working for you and in order to hit the ball you must use the club like a lever, putting pressure on the side of the shaft with your hands.

What causes the debilitating tension that prevents many golfers from taking a practice swing with a ball in the way? I don't mean to sound melodramatic, but it's fear—fear of hitting a poor shot, fear of looking foolish or, perhaps, fear of letting a partner down. You've hit good shots before, but you're never sure when you'll hit the next one because you don't understand exactly how to hit them in the first place.

The antidote for that fear is the confidence that comes from knowing exactly what you need to do in order to hit a good shot and knowing that you've got a damn good chance of doing it, too. When you reach that level of play, this game is really fun. And to build that confidence, the first step is understanding centrifugal force, the bedrock principle upon which good swings are built.

Summary

Centrifugal force, in the special sense that I use the term, is the bedrock principle of good ball-striking. When applied to the swing, it provides everything—power, accuracy, and repeatability. Centrifugal force is generated in the lower body with a hip turn and transmitted through the passive linkage of the arms and hands to the club head, where it takes the form of speed. Its beneficial effects can be ruined by pushing on or applying pressure to the side of the club shaft with the hands and arms. To resist the instinctive urge to do that, think of the club as a rope with a rock tied to the end.

APPLICATION

*"That can't be right! I didn't feel like
I did anything."*

When asked to name the most common problem that I've encountered through the years, I answer without hesitation, "Upper-body tension." Stress in the hands, arms, and shoulders ruins the effects of centrifugal force, and almost invariably, much of my first lesson with a new student is spent trying to get him or her to relax.

Several years ago, I worked with a woman at the Country Club of Orlando who was quick to tell me she'd taken lessons from just about every teaching professional of any reputation from Key West, Florida, to Glasgow, Scotland. None, however, had been able to cure her problem, which was a lack of distance. She said that she'd heard some complimentary things about me and had called for a lesson, but from her tone it was clear that she didn't have much hope.

I asked her to hit some range balls while I watched. She was fit, in her late thirties or early forties, so there was no physical reason for her lack of distance. Apparently, the money she'd spent on all those lessons hadn't been a total waste, because she had a reasonably good idea of what she was supposed to do with the club. Her problem was upper-body tension. She was gripping the club so tightly that her knuckles were white; I could even see veins standing out in her forearms and neck. It was as if she was trying to choke old Mr. Centrifugal Force to death. Tight almost to the point of rigidity, she labored to hit head-high 3-wood shots that barely carried seventy-five yards in the air. I doubt if she could have gotten a shot with her driver off the ground.

On a hunch, I reached in her bag and pulled out a couple of

clubs. Just as I had suspected, there were slick spots on the relatively new grips. So I told her that the first thing she needed to do was relax. Then, with her permission, I massaged the knots of tension from her arms and shoulders. Next, I got behind her and tried to turn her hips. Frankly, I would have had an easier time turning the golf cart parked nearby. She felt as rooted as a tree trunk.

After that, I got her to waggle the club a few times, just to see if her wrists were loose and not cemented together. Then I told her to try again. "I don't care where it goes," I said. "Just take a swing and let the club and ball get in each other's way. And smile at the ball for a change. That grimace isn't working."

The results were dramatic. Her next shot sailed about 150 yards in the air with a high trajectory. There was even a little draw at the end. It really was a fine shot.

Probably feeling a little smug, I asked, "Well, what do you think of that?"

Her reply was a complete surprise. "That can't be right!" she said with a scowl. "I didn't feel like I did anything."

At that point, I began to see the real problem, the underlying one.

"Well, if it feels like you're doing something, then you're probably doing too much. It's not manual labor. You're not chopping wood or breaking rocks with a hammer. It's a swing, a relaxed swing, not a hit. Your arms and hands should feel like they're just hanging off your shoulders. All you do is hold on to the club lightly and swing it back and forth by turning your lower body."

It took a few moments, but when that sank in, she said, "You know, I may have been holding the club too tight."

"Yes, ma'am, you may be on to something there."

Not long ago, a Formula 1 driver came to me for a lesson. After a few shots, I could tell that grip pressure was a problem. Taking his hands and arms, however, I had no difficulty carrying him up to the top and cocking his wrists. It was only as I was bringing him down that I felt tension and resistance.

From experience, I know that when players tighten up on the downswing, it's usually from a fear that they won't have control at impact. So they try to steer the club into the ball and end up ruining the shot. I told him that to release the club properly, he had to feel almost as if he had no control, as if his downswing was uninhibited and he was just "freewheeling" it through the ball.

Hearing that, he recalled something that had happened to him when he'd just started racing and was taking driving instruction. He said that when approaching a curve, his first reaction was always to brake. However, his instructor told him that was the time "to keep the pedal to the metal"; otherwise he'd go into a skid.

In his mind, something similar was happening on the downswing. He was braking and skidding as he approached impact rather than accelerating and letting the club head swing freely through the ball. Once he made the association, a big door opened mentally and his ball-striking improved immediately.

You control the direction of the shot with the proper grip and stance, and you control its distance with your turn. Hand manipulation in a centrifugal-force swing is like braking and skidding in a curve. Through impact, you want to keep the pedal to the metal.

Recently I worked with a new student in Las Vegas who is a good athlete, a former boxer, in fact, but he had a horrible slice. A weak grip was a big part of the problem. After I taught him how to hold the club correctly, his big slice quickly became a little cut. Every second or third shot even flew perfectly straight. However, none of them had the resonance of a shot solidly struck, and they weren't flying as high as I thought they should.

Now, a "thin-sounding" shot with a lower-than-normal trajectory is usually the result of tension in the hands, arms, and shoulders. Tension in the upper body hinders your ability to swing the club freely with centrifugal force. That, in turn, slows the club head, and club-head speed is one of the determining factors of trajectory.

I told my new student that he might be gripping too tightly. That's where upper-body tension usually starts—in the grip. He replied that it felt as if he was holding the club so lightly already that it was about to fly out of his hand at impact.

Well, we were alone on the driving range at the time, no one around to get hurt, so I told him to just let it fly out one time. And that's what he did. He took a swing and let the club go. After we retrieved it, his shots sounded much better, flying higher and straighter than before.

"You know, there are different degrees of tension," he said, later. "I really thought I was holding the club lightly until you showed me what light really is."

It's golf's greatest paradox—you would expect a forced increase in arm speed to increase your power and distance, yet it often does just the opposite. When you consciously try to use your upper body to hit the ball, you ignore the principal source of power in your swing, which is the lower body. You also create tension in your hands, arms, and shoulders, which further hinders your ability to put centrifugal force to work.

Remember—swing the club head with your freely turning lower body while your hands and arms serve as passive linkage.

HOLDING THE CLUB

All of the fundamentals I teach are important, but the way you hold the club is first among equals. It's your only connection to the club, and it's with the club that you hit the ball. Tommy Armour said it was the basic factor of playing good golf, and I agree.

However, if this fundamental were a criminal at large with its picture on the post office wall, one of its aliases would be "The Grip." That's an unfortunate name, but just about everyone who's ever given a golf lesson has used it, me included.

Why do I have a problem with the word "grip"? Because when people think of it, they usually associate it with words like "clench" or "clutch" or "vise," words with tense and stressful connotations. However, when I use it (and I will, often, since it's so common and convenient), I want you to think of things that are light and relaxed, like the way an artist holds the brush to paint a watercolor or a mother holds her child's hand as they walk in the park. Many swing problems start with incorrect hand position, but too much grip pressure or pressure incorrectly applied can be just as big a bogeyman (pun intended).

Now, let's get down to specifics. There are two elements to

holding the club properly: the positioning of your hands, and grip pressure.

Hand Position

I teach a natural grip, one that naturally or reflexively returns the club face squarely to the ball at impact without hand manipulation or forearm rotation. Unless you have the reaction time of that comic book hero the Flash, you won't be able to fine-tune the alignment of your club during the downswing—things will be happening much too quickly for that. The longer-hitting professionals generate club-head speed in excess of 100 mph (some over 120), and many amateurs attain speeds of 80 to 90 mph. Consider also that on a two-hundred-yard shot, a 2-degree error in club-face alignment can cause a twenty-yard miss, and I'm sure you can understand why I prefer a grip that naturally returns the club face squarely.

Of course, the more natural the motion, the easier it is to repeat. That's one of the reasons why almost all of the top players, and I'm talking about the ones who have endured for years and years, have natural grips. Early in their careers, each found a way to hold the club that worked naturally with his or her own physique, a way that made hitting the ball with square, solid contact relatively simple.

To find your own natural grip, always begin with the left hand, because the left arm and the club shaft make up your golfing pendulum.

First, let your left arm hang naturally by your side. Don't clap your hand against your thigh like a soldier at attention. Don't turn it or twist it either. Just let it hang there relaxed. If you're like *most* people, you'll find that your left hand turns in slightly, or, in other words, the palm faces your hip pocket.

Second, curl the last three fingers slightly as if you were about to pick up a suitcase. Without changing the hand's alignment, grip the club with your left hand, making sure that the leading edge of the club face is soled square (perpendicular) to the target line. The club should fit into the "groove" formed by the curled fingers.

Let your left arm hang naturally.

Grip the club with your left arm at your side.

Last, close your palm down over the grip. Make sure the club is held in your fingers and not your palm. That's important.

A good way to double-check your left-hand alignment is to stand relaxed with your body parallel to the intended line of flight of the ball, then lean forward slightly from the waist and allow your arms to dangle in front of you. Now see where the back of your left hand is facing (or the logo on your golf glove, if you're wearing one). With most people, the back of the left hand will face somewhere to the *right* of the target, but everybody's different.

Bring the club around in front.

The right hand comes in from the side.

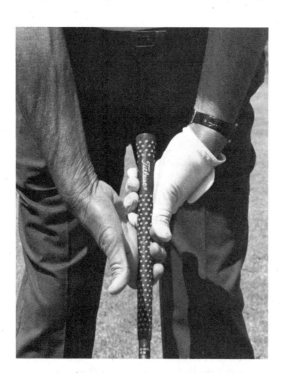

**The club is held
in the fingers.**

Now for the right hand.

There are three variations or "styles" of grips, and all involve the positioning of the left index finger and the right little finger. In my descending order of preference, they're the overlapping or Vardon grip, the ten-finger or baseball grip, and the interlocking grip.

Because the overlapping grip is the one I recommend and the one most people use anyway, I'll begin with it.

Bring the club around in front, still holding it with your natural left-hand grip. Curl the fingers of your right hand and, placing the right hand below the left on the grip, cradle the club in the fingers of your right. Don't reach under the shaft, however, because you'll tend to get the club against the right palm, and that's a mistake. Instead, bring your right hand in from the side. That will help you make sure the club is held in the fingers.

Next, lift the little finger of your right hand and slide your right hand up so that the right ring finger is snug against the left index finger. Then lower the right pinky into the notch between the second knuckles of the left index and middle fingers. With the left thumb fitting neatly into the hollow of the heel of the right hand, close the right palm down over the left thumb.

The left thumb fits into the hollow of the heel of the right hand.

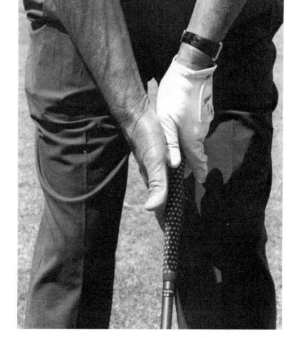

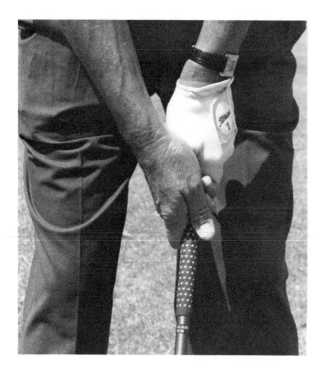

The palm of the right hand should always face the target.

The palm of the right hand should always line up with the leading edge of the club. In other words, it should face the target, much the same as if you were hitting a handball shot. You don't want the palm of your right hand either under the shaft, facing upward, or on top of it, facing downward.

If you prefer a ten-finger or baseball grip, simply leave the little finger of your right hand on the shaft. The ten-finger grip is my second choice if you don't like the overlapping grip.

I'm no fan of the interlocking grip, especially for people with small hands, because it tends to push the club into the palm of the right hand. That not only hinders the natural hinging of the wrists but puts too much of the right *hand* on the club. The more right hand on the club, the more it will want to take an active role during the swing. You should hold the club in your fingers. If the interlocking grip gives you the best results, however, then use it, but try the others first. The interlocking grip is the same as the overlapping grip except the right little finger and the left index finger are interlaced or interlocked.

Now to our second element.

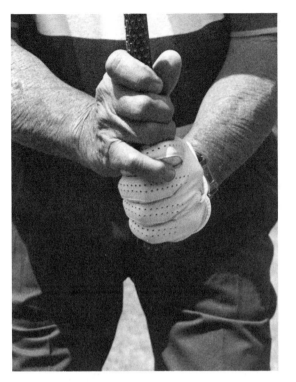

The overlapping grip.

The ten-finger grip.

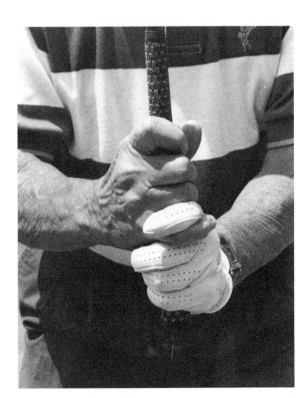

The interlocking grip.

Grip Pressure

Overall, you should exert only enough pressure with your hands to hold the club securely. Exert any more than that and you'll sacrifice club-head speed and the square application of that speed.

If 10 represents the tightest you can squeeze the club and 0 is when it falls out of your hands, then your overall grip pressure at address should be about 4. The club head should actually feel a little heavy. If that grip seems too light, be aware that you will unconsciously increase the pressure to about 6 by impact.

More important, you should hold the club primarily with the little finger of the left hand and the index finger of the right hand. Think of them as bookends, keeping everything snug in between. Because little fingers are usually wimps, your left one will probably need some support from its two stronger neighbors, ring finger and middle finger. As for the other fingers and the two thumbs, they're just along for the ride, especially the thumbs.

Graphically, this is how it should feel:

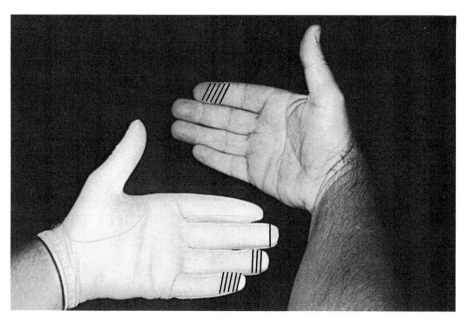

Hold the club primarily with the little finger of your left hand and the index finger of your right.

For most people, the little finger of the left hand is seldom used in life, but it's role in the golf swing is crucial, because it's the base of our golf-club pendulum. Check your glove for signs of wear at the root of the little finger. If you see any, it means you're not holding the club securely enough with it, and that's probably because your little finger is too weak. Hitting practice shots with the correct pressure will strengthen it over time, but if you want to accelerate the process, buy some Silly Putty to squeeze or knead a wet washrag with your left pinky. I'm not particular about how you do it, but if you're like most of the players I work with, you'll need to develop some strength in your left pinky.

It will also help to avoid holding the club all the way up on the end. Leave a little space between your left little finger and the "bell" or butt of the grip. The reason is that the bell is always thicker than the rest of the grip and it's more difficult for the little finger to hold it securely.

Here's a good way to check for the ideal grip pressure in the left hand. First, assume your natural left-hand grip, then, with the right hand, try to turn the club face. Start with the lightest possible pressure in the left hand. If the club slips in your fingers, then gradually increase the pressure until you find the least amount of finger pressure that will keep the club from slipping.

I mentioned above that the thumbs were along for the ride. That's because you must always avoid putting pressure on the side of the shaft, and the thumbs are potentially the worse offenders. Use them actively and you'll ruin any chance of making a good centrifugal-force swing. However, it's also important that the left thumb not slip or slide up and down the grip, especially at the top of the backswing. Again, check your golf glove. If you find signs of wear on the left thumb, then I'd suggest you apply a slight downward pressure with the heel of the right palm to keep the left thumb in place.

Why exert the most pressure primarily with the left little finger and the right index finger?

After many years of experimenting, I've decided it's the lightest grip that still holds the club securely and prevents it from twisting during the swing. You don't want the club to twist in your hands for an obvious reason—it would ruin the shot. The club face would no longer be aligned toward the target at impact and you would strike the ball a weak, glancing blow with a great loss of power.

But why a light grip?

There are a number of reasons and, directly or indirectly, they all have to do with the elimination of a most pervasive golfing enemy—tension.

During the swing, tension hinders the proper functioning of your various anatomical parts; it stifles your ability to sense what those parts are doing. And it also limits the quick but smooth movement of those parts essential for hitting powerful and accurate shots.

A strained grip sets off a chain reaction of tension that goes up the arms and down through the body. Tension in the hips restricts their range of motion and limits the degree to which the shoulders will turn. A restricted shoulder turn reduces the amount of power you can generate. Tense arms won't swing freely. Tense wrists won't cock or hinge fully at the top of the backswing, nor will they uncock and release freely at impact. I could go on, but I won't belabor the point.

When played well, golf is a game of sensations and feel, not of robot mechanics. Tension decreases your ability to feel what happens during the swing, and that's especially true as it relates to the lower body. You generate power with your lower body, and you need to be able to feel your feet, knees, and hips if you're to do it properly. A taut upper body shuts off that communication.

Tension also hinders your ability to move quickly, a very important factor if you want to hit the ball a long way. Tight muscles are slow muscles.

Bobby Jones once said that most golfers would play better if they only understood the proper role of the club shaft. The club shaft should be used to impart velocity to the club head, not to transmit physical force to the ball. He said that the length of a drive depends on the speed of the club head rather than the brute force that bends crowbars and lifts heavy weights. Tight muscles and brute force are two sides of the same coin.

What are the benefits of a light grip?

First and foremost, a light grip helps eliminate tension. While a light grip isn't the only condition for achieving the proper degree of relaxation, it is an essential one.

A soft touch on the club helps loosen the upper body so that the shoulders turn easily, the arms swing freely, and the wrists cock fully. You're also more sensitive to the movement of your hips and legs and can better react to this movement with your upper body. Of course, the more relaxed you are, the quicker you can move, the more club-head speed you can generate, and the farther you can hit the ball.

It's important to start with a light grip and *maintain* it throughout the swing. That isn't easy. As I mentioned earlier, you will instinctively squeeze the club as you change directions at the top. Starting with a light grip, however, increases the chances that your instinctive tightening of the hands won't be enough to inhibit your release at impact. Start with tense hands, though, and it's like slamming on the brakes of a car going uphill!

I don't think I can overstate the importance of a light, natural grip. If you learn how to hold the club properly and how to address the ball (our next fundamental), you've got a real chance at playing consistently decent golf. You may not win the Masters, but you won't embarrass yourself either. However, with a bad grip you'll never play consistent golf.

When a player with a good grip and stance has a bad day, it's probably because he's too tight and too tense. But a person with a bad grip can be relaxed or downright limp—and it's still going to be a struggle from the first swat. That's because he has to do too much with his hands.

A golfer who has a good grip and other good fundamentals and is also relaxed feels as if he's doing everything with his feet, legs, and hips. His upper body is simply reacting to his lower body. But a golfer with a bad grip must actively use his hands, arms, and shoulders, and in the process, he neglects his lower body. The results are inconsistent shots and a lack of power.

I hope I've made my point that good golf starts with a good grip. I know it's not a particularly exciting topic, but it is vitally important. This next section is also about the grip, but in a different context, one that's more historical than instructional. However, there's something to be learned from it, as well.

Weak vs. Strong Grips—
a Moving Scale

When I started playing the game, almost all the good players had what is *now* called a "strong" grip. I say *now* because back then no one called it that. It was just "the grip" or "a natural grip." According to current terminology, you have a strong grip if your left hand is more on top of the club at address than to the side and if when looking down you can see two or even three knuckles on the left hand.

Another way of describing it is to check the V's formed by your thumbs and forefingers. If the V's point toward your right shoulder, that's considered a strong grip today. (I don't necessarily agree with that definition, but we'll get to that in a moment.)

Harry Vardon, Bobby Jones, Walter Hagen, Tommy Armour, Peter Thomson, Billy Casper, and Sam Snead all held the club that way. Gene Sarazen could see all four knuckles on his left hand at address! I could easily fill this page with the names of golf's elite from the turn of the century through the 1950s and into the 1960s who used a strong grip.

Why did they choose to hold the club that way? Because they played better, of course. What other reason could there be? You don't think they held it that way to make the game more difficult, do you?

However, starting in late 1950s, the so-called strong grip fell out of fashion and golfers everywhere began weakening their grips. By that I mean they turned their hands to the left on the club so that the V's pointed more in the direction of the chin than the right shoulder.

Ours is a world of cause and effect, and things don't happen without reasons. In this case, the big reasons were a couple of "impact" players. They held the club with the V's pointing at the chin, so a lot of players thought this must be the universal template for good play, the elusive secret that would cure their golfing woes. Well, like all the other secrets that had come along before, this one wasn't the panacea, either. For many, it only made their problems worse. But before the pendulum of change (not our golfing pendulum) had stopped swinging in the other direction, things got a little bizarre.

One highly publicized modern method of the early 1970s stated that everybody should place the left thumb on top of the shaft at twelve o'clock. Try it sometime. You'll see that the V of your left hand points in the direction of your *left* shoulder. Now, there are a lot of golfers in this world and I'm sure there are

The left hand's position in a highly publicized grip of the early 1970s. Maybe natural for some, but not many.

some who can play quite well with such a grip. Me? I couldn't break 100 holding the club like that, and chances are you couldn't either!

People frowned when they saw somebody else's V's pointing in the direction of the right shoulder. (Some still do.) When they said "strong grip," their noses wrinkled as if it gave off a strong odor. Whew! (Okay, so I'm exaggerating, but I'm not exaggerating much.)

Fortunately, that old pendulum is swinging back now, and it's for the best, in my opinion. Today when I walk the practice tee at PGA Tour events I see more strong grips than weak ones. Percentage-wise, the disparity is even greater on the LPGA Tour. Golf commentators aren't talking much about it yet, and golf writers aren't writing about it, either. But there's a quiet revolution going on out there with the way the game's best players are holding the club. Why? Because they're going back to what works best.

Now, before anyone gets confused, let me say that I do not teach a strong grip. As I stated at the beginning of this chapter, I teach a natural grip. So, why am I glad to see more and more people playing with strong grips these days? *Because what has been labeled a strong grip is, in fact, a natural grip for most golfers.*

For the sake of clarity, perhaps I should digress for a moment and talk about what these labels mean in terms of how they affect the flight of the ball. Please understand that I don't have a big problem with the labels themselves. They're descriptive, and most golfers have some idea what they mean. My disagreement is with their application in individual cases.

To give you a frame of reference, I'll start by describing the natural grip and how it affects the ball's flight. Please assume a good swing and passive hands with the following examples.

As I said earlier, a natural grip is one that automatically returns the club face squarely to the back of the ball at impact. All of the kinetic energy built up during the swing is transferred to the ball. The club face imparts some backspin (the amount varies from club to club), and the ball flies on a trajectory that is normal for the loft of the club used. The overall result is a straight, powerful shot and, of course, that's what most golfers want.

A strong grip returns the club face to the ball "shut" or "hooded." By that, I mean the club face is aligned left of the target, so the ball is struck a glancing blow—with several consequences. First, right-to-left sidespin is imparted and the ball usually curves to the left. Second, overspin is imparted (or at least there's little backspin), so when the ball lands, it rolls on like a wheel. Third, the club is de-lofted (a 5-iron becomes a 4-iron, in effect) and the ball flies lower. The overall result is a low-flying shot that curves to the left and rolls a lot when it lands. Usually, that combination means a longer shot, and that's why it's called a strong grip. Now, in order to hit a straight shot with a strong grip, you must consciously inhibit the natural action of your hands so that the club face remains square at impact. That's not easy to do on a consistent basis.

A weak grip is the opposite of a strong grip. With a weak grip, the club face returns to the ball "open," or facing to the right of the target. Left-to-right sidespin is imparted and the ball usually curves right. The club's loft is increased (a 5-iron becomes a 6-iron, in effect), so the ball flies higher than you would expect with that particular club and tends to stop more quickly when it lands. The overall result is a high-flying shot that curves to the right and doesn't roll much. Obviously, the reason it's called a weak grip is that it usually produces a shorter shot. In order to hit a straight shot with a weak grip, you must consciously roll your hands and forearms (actively turn them to the left) so that the club face is square at impact. In my opinion, it's even more difficult to consistently hit a straight shot with a weak grip than with a strong one.

Why would someone want to use anything other than a natural grip? I can think of two reasons, neither of which has much merit, in my opinion.

First, some players alter their grips (that is, make them weaker or stronger) to curve shots that better fit the shape of a particular hole, or a course, or the weather conditions, or even the player's own personality. For the advanced golfer, that can be a worthwhile goal, but I don't approve of the means. Except for a few short finesse shots from around the green, I don't think you should alter your grip.

Second, less skillful players often weaken or strengthen their grips to compensate for deficiencies in their swings. For example, a chronic slicer might strengthen his grip in hopes of hitting straight shots, or at least less crooked ones. He's usually disappointed at the result, however, because on the golf course, as everywhere else, two wrongs don't make a right.

Now let's get back to the matter of where your V's should point so that the club automatically squares up to the target line at impact. That's really what we're after, isn't it?

Is there some universal standard? Should every golfer hold the club with the V's pointing at the chin, or at the right shoulder, or perhaps somewhere in between, like the right ear? Should your grip look like Paul Azinger's or anyone else's?

To all those questions, the answer is simply *no*.

We're all different. There's a world of variation in the human anatomy, and every physique is unique. Some of us are tall, some of us short, some thick, some thin. Of particular importance to golfers is the size of their hands and the length of their fingers, because those two factors (which vary greatly) significantly affect where the V's point.

If you were a haberdasher, would you try to sell the same size sport coat to every customer? Of course not. A 42 regular might fit some, but it wouldn't fit everybody. So you would take measurements and give each customer a custom fit. Well, the golf grip, just like a sport coat, needs some tailoring, too.

For the individual, strong and weak can only be determined after establishing what's natural for that person. In terms of where the V's point, it's a moving scale, and it depends on three factors: hand size, finger length, and the alignment of your left hand in relation to the target when you allow your left arm to hang relaxed at your side.

So where should the V's point with your natural grip? At the chin? The right shoulder? Somewhere in between?

There's no universal template, but there is a method for determining it in each case, and I demonstrated it for you at the beginning of this chapter. My recommendation is that you find out what's natural for you and stick with it. You'll play better, and more consistently. Don't move your hands around just to position them as someone else does.

A word of caution to the golfer who has followed my advice to determine his natural grip and discovered that with his *right* hand facing the target it's in a stronger position than before:

Short-term, expect to hit some hooks.

You'll hit them not because of your new grip, but because of a bad habit you acquired to compensate for the deficiencies of your old grip. Like all bad habits, this one will take time to get rid of.

If, with that old grip, you managed to hit the ball straight, then you've been actively rotating your hands and forearms, whether you realized it or not. You've had to. Otherwise, it would be one slice after another. Now you'll need to retrain your upper body to remain passive and let the way God assembled you square up the club face at impact.

If you're a better player and your right hand has been on top of the club, your big complaint has probably been a lack of consistency. You hit good shots for a few holes, maybe even for a round. Then, on the back nine or the next day, the magic just disappears. The reason is that with your old grip, you had to rely heavily on hand-eye coordination, which, just like biorhythms, fluctuates.

However, with a natural grip and the swing I teach, you don't need much, if any, hand-eye coordination. You may be surprised to hear that, but it's true. I know because I teach several blind golfers, and hand-eye coordination is something they just don't have. They still play quite well, however, all things considered.

Now, another word of caution, this one to the golfer who followed my advice for determining his natural grip and discovered that with his *right* hand facing the target it's in a weaker position than before:

Short-term, expect to hit some shots to the right.

The culprit here is excessive grip pressure. In order to hit a straight shot with your old grip, you had to choke off your release to keep the club face square through impact. The cure in your case is to eliminate tension in the upper body, especially in the hands and wrists. Holding the club primarily in the fingers will help a lot.

In my opinion, this is the easier of the two problems to fix. It's also the problem that periodically bothers me. Because I don't want to unload early, I sometimes inhibit the release with a little extra grip pressure, and the result is a block.

I'm sure you've noticed that in the last several paragraphs, I've referred only to the *right* hand. That's because, in my opinion, it's the right hand, not the left, that primarily determines club-face alignment at impact.

These days, however, most people who see a grip with several knuckles of the left hand showing will usually label it strong and assume that sooner or later it will cause a hooded club face and a hook. But that's not the case. A hooded club face at impact is much more likely to be caused by a strong position not of the left hand but of the right hand, with the right hand underneath the shaft and facing upward.

This misconception probably started because of an instructional trend to position the hands on the club with the palms facing, or opposing one another, like mirror images. Thus, according to that dictum, if the left hand were on top of the club, the right hand would be underneath it and in a strong position, but that's not a natural grip.

With a natural grip, while the left hand's position on the club may vary from player to player, the right palm is always positioned so that it faces the target at address, like an extension of the club's leading edge. Obviously, there are some players whose palms will face like mirror images when using a natural grip, and with many the palms will almost face. However, the driving principle behind the natural grip is *not* to have your palms face, but rather to hold the club so that your anatomy automatically and reflexively squares the club at impact.

If you're wondering, I did not invent the natural grip. You might say I inherited it from my golfing ancestors, from people like Tommy Armour, Percy Boomer, Bobby Jones, Sam Snead, and many others, so it has an excellent pedigree. They held the club that way because it worked for them, and I teach it today because it still works. "Palms facing" sounds nice in theory, and for some it does the job. But a natural grip will do the job for everybody.

Before getting into our summary, I'd like to mention an equipment modification some of you may be using or have thought about using that can have a bad effect on your performance. I'm talking about oversized grips on your clubs.

Unless you have very large hands or suffer from some medical condition like arthritis that keeps you from curling your fingers, I don't recommend using oversized grips. The larger the grip, the more it must rest in the palm and, accordingly, the less your wrists will cock. That's like giving away club-head speed, and most players don't need to do that.

My teacher Tommy Armour wore an extra-large glove, yet his grips were standard, if not a little undersized. Paul Azinger has large hands, but he uses standard-size grips. Most of the players on tour use only one wrapping under their grips so they can hold the club more in their fingers, and that's what I recommend for you.

Summary

A correct grip is crucial, because it's your only connection to the club. I teach a natural grip, one that automatically returns the club face squarely to the ball at impact without hand manipulation or forearm rotation. The essence of a natural grip is the way the back of the left hand aligns in relation to the body and the intended target line. While the appearance of a natural grip may change from player to player, the method of determining it is the same for everyone.

First, let your left arm hang relaxed at your side. The left arm is your "pole star" or point of reference, because it and the club form your golfing pendulum. With the club soled square to the target line, grip it with your left hand in that position. Holding the club in your fingers, close your palm down over the grip.

Move the club around in front and bring your right hand in from the side, placing it on the grip below the left hand. The club is cradled in the fingers of the right hand. With the left thumb fitting neatly into the hollow of the heel of the right palm, close the right hand down over the left. Your right palm should face the target like an extension of the leading edge of the club.

My first preference is the overlapping grip, followed by the ten-finger grip. I don't recommend the interlocking grip, because it tends to position the club in the palms, thus hindering a full wrist cock.

Concerning grip pressure, the club should be held primarily with two fingers—the left little finger and the right index finger. Because little fingers are usually weak, the ring finger and middle fingers of the left hand are used in a supporting role. Overall, you should hold the club lightly, exerting just enough firmness to control it and keep it from twisting.

Don't alter the position of your hands. Use a natural grip with every club on every shot.

APPLICATION

"I'll hook the ball off the planet with this grip!"

Back in 1979, my son Bo, who was caddying on the LPGA Tour at the time, called me one night from somewhere on the road.

"Dad, one of the girls out here is looking for a teacher," he said. "She was wondering if you would work with her."

"What's her name?"

"Muffin Spencer-Devlin."

"Hmmm."

"You know who she is, don't you?"

"Oh, yes."

"Well?"

"Son, give me a minute. I need to think about it."

It wasn't an easy decision. A few weeks before, I had watched Muffin play at the Lady Citrus in Orlando. She is a fine athlete and an attractive young woman, but I wasn't sure that working with her was such a good idea. In Orlando, I'd seen her do yoga exercises on the course and lean against trees and talk to them. Some people march to a different drummer, but at the time, I thought Muffin was hearing another percussion section.

Frankly, I don't know why I said yes. I guess my son caught me at a weak moment, but I'm glad he did. Today, Muffin is a dear friend. However, the relationship didn't start out very smoothly.

She and I met for the first time several weeks later. "Are you willing to do what I tell you to do?" I asked, having no intention of putting up with any foolishness. "Otherwise I'll be wasting your time and you'll be wasting mine."

"Maybe. Maybe not," she replied, not backing up an inch. "I want to hear what you have to say first."

"This may be the quickest lesson you've ever had," I muttered.

In the middle of my driving range, there was an old tractor tire about eighty yards away. I'd left it there because it made an excellent target. A 15-mph wind was blowing toward us that morning.

"Hit some wedges and aim for the tire," I told her.

Well, after about seven or eight of these pitiful "dying quails" that flew out about fifty yards, then fell down to the right, I couldn't stand it any longer.

"Give me that club!"

I took her wedge, moved the ball back in my stance, and on the first swing, without warming up, hit the tire with a low-trajectory shot that never left the line.

"Is that the way you want to hit it?"

She nodded. "Yeah. Teach me."

"Okay, I will, provided you do everything I say."

She replied with a look that said, "Well, I don't know about that!"

So I told her that she had to be the world's greatest putter.

After she conceded that she was a good putter, I said, "Otherwise, with that swing, I don't see how you ever got on the tour."

Sometimes you have to say things like that to get their attention. Fortunately, she took it the right way. She grinned, I grinned, then we called a truce and got on with the lesson.

The first thing I changed was her grip. Her left thumb was actually to the left of center on the shaft and her right hand was on top of the shaft. She was tight and very "handsy," because with that extremely weak grip she had to rotate her hands and forearms hard to square the club face at impact. I showed her how to hold it naturally with her left hand on the club the way it hung by her side relaxed and with her right on it so that the palm faced the target.

She took one look and said, "I'll hook the ball off the planet with this grip!"

Well, Muffin may know more about things extraterrestrial than I do, but I know more about grips. So I moved the ball back in her stance and told her just to hit it.

She had a good swing, in spite of what I'd told her, so I wasn't surprised when the ball left on a low trajectory and missed the tire by about five yards to the right. It was actually drawing a little at the end, heading for the tire. Vindication is always worth something, but the look of disbelief on her face was priceless. I don't think she'd ever hit a shot like that in her life. However, before we'd finished that lesson, she was whistling one "knockdown" wedge after another at my old tractor tire.

Today, I think back to that morning and know it was a watershed in Muffin's golfing life. When she learned to hold the club naturally, she took an important step on the road to becoming a player of note and a tournament winner on the LPGA Tour. Sometimes you can make a difference, and that's why I love to teach.

STANDING TO THE BALL

Everyone is capable of taking a good stance, just as everyone is capable of holding the club correctly. The first two fundamentals are actually just preliminaries for what's to follow. Because they don't have any moving parts, they're the easiest to learn, too. You could say they're the "paint-by-number" fundamentals of the swing. However, get these two right and your chances of hitting good shots will increase dramatically.

There are four elements to standing to the ball correctly—posture, alignment, ball position, and weight distribution.

Posture

Golf is a physical sport and, like other physical sports, it should be played from an athletic stance. Imagine yourself as a linebacker or a shortstop. What would you do to get ready for the next snap or the next pitch?

Wouldn't you spread your feet, flex your knees, lean forward from the waist, and let your arms hang down naturally? Sure you would. You do about the same thing if you were playing basketball or tennis or volleyball, too, almost any sport, really, because from this stance you're balanced and ready to move, ready to act and react with quickness and power.

Golf is no different. And like other sports, golf is played primarily with the lower body.

A pitcher throws a baseball with his legs, not his arm, just as a boxer throws a punch with his legs, not his arm. That may come as a surprise to some of you, but it shouldn't. Why do prizefighters do so much roadwork in preparation for a fight? Sure, they're building stamina, but they're also strengthening their legs so they can punch harder. Why do pitchers report to spring training earlier than their teammates? For conditioning, of course, and it's mainly for their legs. It's the lower body that sends the message—the upper body just delivers it.

But let's look at it a little differently. How hard do you think that boxer could hit you if he were standing on a block of ice? Do you think the pitcher could make a strong and accurate throw to home plate if he were suspended several inches above the ground with a harness and wire? If you put the boxer on ice and hang the pitcher in air, you've taken their legs away from them. Ever tried to play a round of golf wearing street shoes with slick soles? That should give you some idea.

You play golf with your lower body, just as people play other sports, and accordingly, you should use another athletic activity—walking—for guidance in finding the proper stance.

Why walking? Well, it's something most of us are familiar with, for starters. When you walk, you're balanced and your knees are flexed. You lean forward slightly from the waist and your arms swing freely from the shoulders, just as you do in that athletic stance I talked about a few paragraphs ago.

Your normal walking pace provides another important key as well—*the width of your stance when hitting a driver should be the length of a normal pace*. You may have heard of a different measure for determining how far a golfer should spread his feet, the width of his shoulders, but that one has always confused me. I've never known whether it was measured from the inside of the feet or the outside, and it does make a difference. For instance, my feet are each about three and a half inches wide. Multiply that by two and the product is seven inches. That's a big difference when it comes to positioning your feet to hit a golf ball.

If your stance is too wide, a common fault, the level, free turning of your hips will be hindered. You'll have to either sway in order to use your lower body or tilt your hips rather than turn them. Swaying moves your head and spine laterally, altering the path of the club head and making hitting good golf shots more difficult. Remember the washer-and-string demonstration from the chapter on centrifugal force? If your hips tilt or lift, the result is usually a shot hit fat or a high, weak slice. That's because tilting your hips causes an abrupt up-and-down chopping action. It robs you of power because it reduces the width of the club head's arc.

It's better to have too narrow a stance than one too wide. Bobby Jones won thirteen major championships with a stance not much wider than the span of one hand. He thought the feet should be, in his own words, "just far enough apart to accommodate a little footwork when the body was turned from side to side." For most people, "just far enough apart" with a driver is the length of a normal walking pace.

With the other clubs, narrow your stance slightly in increments as they get shorter. Rather than tell you exactly how much, I'd prefer to leave that for your determination on the practice tee. I'm sure you will strike them better with a more compact stance.

Your weight should be evenly distributed between your heels and the balls of your feet, as if you were dancing. The concern here is maintaining your balance while swinging, so you never want to be out on your toes.

Align your feet in relation to each other, naturally. When addressing the ball, position them the same way they would point if you were walking or standing at the back fence talking to a neighbor. Do they line up parallel to one another, or do they splay out a little, like a duck's feet? Most people's toes angle outward slightly, mine included. I know that some teachers advo-

With the driver, your stance should be the width of a normal pace. As the clubs get shorter, your stance gets narrower.

Stance with a 5-iron.

cate a "toed-in" back foot, but I think my method is better.

If your feet naturally point outward, then toeing in your right foot creates tension as you swing the club back. Tension anywhere in the body prior to the change of direction at the top of the swing encourages hitting from the top. Some say you should align the right foot perpendicular (at a right angle) to the target line, then coil or wind the upper body against the lower body

Stance with a 7-iron.

Stance with a pitching wedge.

like a spring. I don't agree. You can hit the ball just as far, as accurately, and as consistently without the extra stress.

There is a moment of tension in the swing I teach, but it's generated and released so quickly you'll hardly notice. It doesn't encourage hitting from the top, but rather provides insurance against it. This tension is the dynamic creation of the upper body and lower body moving in opposite directions at the same time—the hips are starting forward to the ball, initiating the downswing, while the shoulders, arms, and hands are still swinging the club up to complete the backswing. I'll discuss it later in detail, but it's important to understand that this is different from artificially turning in your right foot to create tension from the very beginning of the backswing.

How far should you stand from the ball at address? As close as you can with your arms still able to swing freely from side to side. And how close is that? It depends on your physique. By taking your athletic stance, however, you should be able to find the proper distance easily.

Bend forward from the waist slightly, keeping your knees flexed, then let your arms dangle and see how much space separates your hands and body. If you're like most people, your

For most players, the butt of the club should be a hand's width from the body.

hands will hang about a hand's width from the front of your thighs. That's about how far the butt of the club should be from your body when you address the ball. If you have a thick torso or a large chest, you may need to stand farther away to free up your arms.

Check it out on the practice tee and find the best distance for you, but remember to stand close to the ball, because that promotes an upright swing plane. At first it may feel as if you're crowding it, but you'll probably be surprised at just how close you can get to the ball and still hit good golf shots. The one thing we don't want to do is reach for the ball.

Reaching for the ball causes three major problems. First, it creates tension throughout your body, and in particular in the hands and arms. Second, it restricts the ability of your hips to turn. Third, it flattens your swing plane, which encourages the active use of your hands and also reduces the distance that the club face is perpendicular to and moving along the target line at impact. I don't know which of these is worse, but they're all poison. However, the antidote is readily available—get closer.

The position of your head is another important factor. At address and throughout the swing, it should be centered between your shoulders. At address, hold it naturally, following the normal curvature of the spine. On the backswing, allow your head to turn some, moving with the shoulders.

I see many older golfers, especially those who wear bifocals, with their chins down on their chests. That's a mistake, because it restricts the shoulder turn. Instead, keep your chin up and just "peep" at the back of the ball with your master eye, as Percy Boomer recommended.

I've covered a lot of material already, so let's have a quick review before moving on.

1.   Use an athletic stance. Stand relaxed with your knees flexed and directly over your ankles, then bend forward slightly from the waist. Your arms should hang comfortably.

2. For balance and lateral stability, spread your feet the length of a normal walking pace when hitting a driver. For shorter clubs, narrow your stance incrementally. Allow your feet to align naturally. If they splay out a little, don't toe them in.

3. Your weight should be evenly distributed between your heels and the balls of your feet. You never want to be out on your toes.

4. Stand as close to the ball as you can with your arms still able to swing freely from side to side. For most players, the butt of the club should be about a hand's span from the front of the thigh.

5. Your head should be centered between your shoulders with your chin up slightly, and you should "peep" at the back of the ball with your master eye. No hard stares!

6. The overall feeling should be one of balance, readiness, and ease of movement.

Alignment

An old and still popular analogy for teaching alignment is a golfer on railroad tracks. He stands on one rail with the ball placed on the other and tries to hit it "down the line." It's an effective image, because it conveys the idea of the golfer aligning his body parallel to the intended target line.

With the club face soled squarely behind the ball, your feet, knees, hips, shoulders, and even your eyes should all be aligned *parallel to the intended target line* and *perpendicular to the club face*. Your knees and hips should be level. Your right shoulder will be slightly lower at address than your left, because your right hand is placed below the left on the grip, but don't exaggerate it. You should have a sense of being parallel to the target line and ready to swing along it. Let me recommend two things which will help achieve that feeling.

First, create your own railroad tracks on the practice tee with a couple of clubs. Lay one down pointing toward the target and

Two clubs laid parallel, like railroad tracks, will help your alignment.

a second club parallel to it, a foot or two nearer to you. Then take your stance, placing your feet where the toes of your shoes are close to the shaft of the second club. With your feet parallel to the target line, it's also easy to align your knees, hips, and shoulders parallel. Hit some practice shots with those two clubs on the ground as an alignment aide. Better yet, make it a regular part of your practice routine. It's a simple but effective way of developing a sense of parallel alignment.

Another technique, one you can use on the course when playing, is to pick out a spot ten inches or so in front of the ball on the target line and use it as a reference. The spot can be a blade of grass, a leaf, a discolored area, anything really, just as long as it helps you line up properly. It makes alignment more exact, because it brings the target in from, say, two hundred yards to a few inches. Actually, it's a technique borrowed from bowling. Not only will it help you make sure your club face is square to the target, but by drawing an imaginary line in your mind from the ball to that spot, you can use that line to make sure your body is parallel.

I've seen many golfers place a club across their chests or stomachs, then sight down it toward the target to check their alignment. The better way to do that is to lay the club across your thighs. That's more accurate because you're working with two thigh surfaces, not with just one stomach surface (and often it's a rounded surface).

These are just simple techniques to help you achieve something that is basically simple itself. But don't let the simplicity of proper alignment lull you into thinking it's unimportant. I prom-

To check your alignment, lay a club across your thighs, not your chest or stomach.

ise you it is not. Over time, even a minor inaccuracy in your alignment will insidiously alter your swing as you unconsciously try to compensate for it. This is one of those cases where an ounce of prevention is worth a pound of cure.

Ball Position

By ball position, I mean where the ball is located in relation to your feet, whether it's closer to the left foot, closer to the right foot, or in the middle. That may not sound like such a big deal, but no less a player than Bobby Jones thought it was one of the vital considerations when hitting a golf ball. He said placing the ball at address should always receive minute attention. I've seen some good swings go on the rocks because of a slight but misguided change in ball position. I've also seen golfers with real potential struggle for years without significant improvement because the ball was placed improperly in their stance.

As a matter of fact, my method of teaching advanced players how to "shape" shots—that is, how to hit fades, draws, low shots, and high ones—is based in large measure on moving the ball in relation to the feet.

With ball position, you want to accomplish two things. First, for all shots except for those struck with a driver, you want the club and ball to "get in each other's way" at the lowest point of the downswing arc. In other words, you want to hit the ball with a *descending* blow. A descending blow imparts backspin which makes the ball fly higher and straighter. It also helps the ball land softer. These things are important if you're to hit accurate iron and fairway wood shots. With the driver, you hit the ball with an *ascending* blow, striking it just after the club head has passed the lowest point of its arc. An ascending blow imparts overspin for distance.

Second, you want to be able to make the same swing with different clubs, realizing, of course, that the swing plane for a shorter club will be more upright than the one for a longer club.

To accomplish these objectives, you must change the position of the ball slightly with each club, because the shaft of each club is different in length.

Use the 7-iron as your point of reference. When hitting shots with it, position the ball directly in the middle of your stance, the same distance from the heel of each foot. For that reason, I call it the middle iron. Its shaft length is about midway between the driver and wedge, too.

As the clubs get shorter, the ball is moved back toward the right foot in half-inch increments, which, in fact, is also the approximate difference in shaft length from club to club. Conversely, as the clubs get longer, the ball is moved in the other direction, forward toward the left foot, in half-inch increments. You can see how my ball position has changed in the photographs on pages 42–43.

For example, if the ball position for a 7-iron shot is in the middle of the stance, then it's a half-inch to the right of center with the 8-iron. With a 5-iron, the ball position is an inch to the left of center, with a 3-iron, two inches left of center. When hitting a driver, the exception, the ball is teed up and played off the left heel, where it's struck on the upswing, thus imparting overspin.

Please note that for the irons, I'm only talking about a range of four inches, approximately the width of the back of your hand, but it does make a difference in terms of hitting the ball flush.

I'm well aware that my position on ball position, so to speak, runs counter to the prevailing theory of playing the ball off the left heel with every club. But the prevailing theory also advocates a deliberate lateral weight shift, and you know my feelings about that. If the ball is played forward in your stance with every club, you have to make a lateral movement to get to it. Or is it the other way around—if you make a lateral movement, you have to play the ball forward? I guess it's the old question of which came first, the chicken or the egg, the weight shift or the forward ball position. Not that it matters, because I don't teach either; they are just unnecessary complications as far as I'm concerned.

If you're skeptical, why not prove my point to yourself by hitting some practice shots with different clubs and changing the position of the ball? Actually, you don't have to hit balls at all. Just make a few swings, preferably without looking down, take some turf, and examine where the divot is in relation to your feet. You see, that's one of the ways I proved it to myself—*by hitting golf balls without looking.*

Years ago, I found that with the ball placed forward in my stance, I could never hit the ball flush with any club if I didn't look at it first. Play the ball forward and you have to look, because you have to move your body laterally to get to it. But with the ball positioned back in my stance, I found that I could hit a bucket of balls with my wedge without looking and not miss one! After I stumbled onto that little revelation, I began experimenting with the other clubs and found that by changing the position of the ball with each, good square contact was easier to attain. The other way I proved it to myself was by teaching blind golfers.

I don't think I've ever done anything quite so rewarding as teaching people with severe vision impairment. I guess we all take a lot for granted, but helping a blind man hit a golf ball and hit it well gave me a great deal of satisfaction, besides a whole new perspective on my own puny problems. It also confirmed my theory on ball position. If a man can't see the ball, you had better place it where his club head finds it automatically, and that's what happens with this method.

By the way, I'm not the first professional to advocate playing the ball in different positions with different clubs. At one time, it was commonly taught, so there's lengthy precedent for it.

Weight Distribution

Because you want to hit the ball with an ascending blow with your driver, the distribution of your weight should favor your right side slightly, say 60 percent on the right foot, 40 percent on the left foot. With the other clubs, reverse that and favor your

With the driver, your weight should favor your right side.

With the other clubs, your weight should favor your left side.

left side *slightly,* to ensure a descending blow. These percentages, however, are just approximations.

But remember—there's no *intentional* weight shift or lateral movement during the swing. The initial distribution of your weight will change some because of the dynamic nature of a good swing. Overall, however, your weight stays centered between the feet until your own momentum pulls you onto your left side. The finish position, though, is the effect of centrifugal force, the cause of which is your hip turn. It is not the product of an intentional weight shift.

Summary

Standing to the ball properly involves four elements: posture, alignment, ball position, and weight distribution.

Walking provides the keys for correct posture. Your knees should be flexed with your weight balanced between the heels and balls of your feet. With your back straight, bend slightly from the waist and allow your arms to hang relaxed from your shoulders. With the driver, the width of your stance is the length of a normal walking pace, and your feet are positioned naturally. With the shorter clubs, your stance is narrowed.

Visualizing a golfer on railroad tracks, align your body parallel to the target line and perpendicular to the club face. Your feet, knees, hips, and shoulders are all parallel to that line. Your feet and hips are level, while your right shoulder is slightly lower than your left.

In order to make the same swing with every club and to let the ball and club face get in each other's way at the bottom of the swing arc, you must change the ball's position with each club. With the 7-iron, the middle iron, the ball is played in the middle of your stance. As the clubs get shorter, move the ball to the right in half-inch increments. As the clubs get longer, move the ball to the left in half-inch increments. With the driver, the ball is teed and played off the left heel.

For shots you intend to hit with a descending blow (that is, all shots *except* the ones that are teed and hit with a driver), your weight should be distributed so as to slightly favor your left side. For the driver, which you want to hit with an ascending blow, favor your right side slightly.

APPLICATION

"Yeah, it looked good, didn't it?"

Several years ago, I made a presentation at a PGA Teaching Summit in Nashville, Tennessee, and stayed with Stuart Smith, one of my students. Stuart's a fine player and was on the tour for a while, but decided he could make a better living back home selling stocks and bonds. While I was there, he asked me to work with a blind friend of his, Dave Meador.

Dave's problem, Stuart told me, was his wedge play, which was keeping him from being a top player. He was shooting scores in the 105–115 range and missing greens with his wedge because he couldn't control his distance with it. I had some free time, so I agreed to help.

We met at a park one morning, and I watched him hit some shots. Stuart would line Dave up by holding the club over the ball and pointing the shaft at the target. Dave would reach out, take the club with both hands, and use it as reference to align his shoulders and hips parallel. Then he would take his grip and Stuart would sole the club squarely behind the ball.

Overall, Dave's fundamentals were good—Stuart had taught him well—so major swing changes weren't required. However, a little fine-tuning was in order, and these were the adjustments I made.

First, I moved the ball back in his stance, instructing Stuart to position it about one and a half inches right of center with the wedge. That would allow the ball and club to get in each other's way when Dave made a pendulum swing, so he wouldn't feel as if he had to "find" the ball with his hands on the way down. He'd had to do that before, and I could see the tension in his hands and forearms.

Second, I narrowed his stance with the shorter clubs, which

made it easier for him to move his lower body. Then, standing behind him, I turned and re-turned his hips level.

"Keep your upper body relaxed, turn your hips like this, and let the club swing," I told him. "Don't try to help it with your hands."

"Yes, sir."

"Okay, your grip's good, the ball's in the right place, and Stuart has you aligned properly. Now hit a few for me."

His first few swings weren't bad, and I could see an expression of surprise on his face. He was making a balanced, level turn with his lower body and the ball was getting in the club's way, just as I'd told him it would.

Then he made a swing that was as pure as mother's love.

"Dave, that was a great shot," I said.

"Yeah, it looked good, didn't it, John?"

I've often wondered what he saw in his mind as I watched that little white ball sail across a blue sky.

It was remarkable how quickly Dave developed a feel for swinging the club with his lower body. And once he started to strike the ball more consistently with his wedge, teaching him how to control distance with it was easy. (I'll show you the same technique in the chapter on pitching.)

But the story doesn't end there. Since then I've made several trips back to Nashville and worked with Dave each time. I've marveled at the continued improvement in his ball-striking. And not long ago, on a cold, blustery day in Phoenix, Arizona, Dave Meador, with Stuart Smith's help, shot a 93 and won the 1992 Heather Farr–Guiding Eyes Classic, by twelve shots! I know Dave's proud of that, but he isn't any prouder of it than I am.

As they walked off the course in Phoenix, Stuart asked Dave how he thought he'd played, and Dave said he thought he could have played a lot better. Is that typical of all golfers after a good round, or what?

If I were blind, I think the scariest thing about playing golf would be trying to hit a ball when I wasn't exactly sure of its location. Trying to find it on the way down, my arms might stray from my body and I would feel that they were disconnected from my turn. But if the ball was positioned at the bottom of my practice-swing arc, I could confidently make a level, stationary pivot with my lower body, letting my arms swing, and know that the club and ball were going to get in each other's way. And with my arms relaxed, they would remain close, so my body would know where they were, so to speak, and my turn would be a connected one.

Paul Azinger probably has the greatest feel for his stance of anyone I've ever taught. When it's perfect, he'll tell me, "This will be a good shot," and it always is. When it's not, however, he can struggle, and more often than not the problems start with too much weight on his right side.

Paul's known as a low-ball hitter, and I attribute that to a couple of things. One, he grew up in south Florida, where the wind blows most of the time. Players who grow up where it's windy, like on the coasts or in Texas, tend to be low-ball hitters. And two, when he's playing well, his weight is about 60 percent on his left side at address, and that, in effect, reduces the loft of his clubs a degree or two.

However, when the Tour moves inland and away from the wind, Paul tends to shift more of his weight onto his back foot so he can hit the ball higher. That's a normal thing to do, but it also changes the way he "sees" the target at address, and over time it will affect his alignment. When I haven't worked with him for a while, that's one of the first things I'll check. If he's been setting up on his right side, I'll usually find he's also aiming to the right.

Now, if that were the only consequence, then it would be a simple fix. However, with his weight on his right side at address, he also tends to bring the club back more inside than normal, and being aimed right, he feels he has to use his hands to help get the club back on line. You never forget where the target is, even with your back to it.

So, because of a desire to hit the ball higher, he changes his weight distribution at address, altering his alignment, which, in turn, affects the planes of both backswing and downswing. As an end result, he'll start trying to steer the ball back to the target with his upper body, which only makes the situation worse. The foundation of his game is lower-body power and control, not upper-body manipulation.

A couple of years ago, I took pictures of his stance when it was perfect. Since then I've used them from time to time to make sure everything was in order. Those should continue to be an excellent reference, provided he doesn't get any taller.

At the beginning of the 1989 season, I drove over to Bradenton, Florida, to work with Paul. Having won a couple of tournaments in 1988, he was preparing to play in the Tournament of Champions at La Costa.

The first thing I noticed was that his stance had gotten wider in the intervening months. When I asked him about it, he said he felt stronger that way, as if he could really rip it with that stance.

My reply was that he couldn't turn as well with a wide stance. He hit several drives to show me, and, of course, they were all long and straight.

"John, I've got to play with this stance."

Sometimes the better part of valor is discretion, as Shakespeare said. After that, I just kept my mouth shut.

The rough is always high at La Costa, so I wasn't totally surprised when I heard Paul opened with a 79 or 80. His second round wasn't much better. However, the more he played, the better he scored, and by Sunday afternoon he'd turned things around completely. After the tournament, I called him.

"You were right," he said. "That stance was too wide."

"I noticed your scores got better. You must have narrowed it some."

"I did, on the twenty-seventh hole. I think I was twelve over by then. After that, I played fine the rest of the way."

Remember—your stance with the driver should never be wider than the length of your normal walking pace. If it's any wider than that, your turn will be affected, and if you can't turn your hips, you won't be able to hit it with your practice swing.

THE TAKEAWAY

With the preliminaries of grip and stance behind us, we can now get down to the business of setting the club in motion. The first segment of the swing is commonly referred to as the takeaway, and that's what I'll call it, although "swingaway" is a more accurate name.

When I was a boy learning to play this game, someone told me that the first eighteen inches of the swing were very important. Today, almost fifty years later, I've yet to experience anything that would make me disagree.

With a good takeaway, you accomplish two things, both of which are vital. First, you fix the proper sequence of moves. In other words, you determine the part of the body initiating the motion and which parts follow and in what order. Second, you establish pace or tempo. Think of it as the swing's pulse. Should it be slow or racing, steady or erratic?

With regard to the first, I want to emphasize, however, that *the good swing is a seamless whole,* not a collection of positions cobbled together, but a continuous movement in which one sensation evolves and flows into the next.

We've learned valuable lessons about this game with high-speed photography and video cameras, but sometimes I fear that because of them we no longer see the forest for the trees. With slow-motion, stop-action, and freeze-frame photography, golfers today tend to think of the swing in terms of static positions, not the dynamic unity it should be. Perhaps that's to be expected, because for a long time that's how the swing has been taught—by isolating what appear to be discernible parts and teaching them separately. There's nothing wrong with that approach *if* the student understands it's the whole he seeks. However, with the new technology, our attention is now riveted on these parts, and that's not how the game is played—at least not how it's played well. (It reminds me of the poem about dissecting the bird to find the song, then wondering why the bird could no longer sing.)

In explaining how you start this flowing and evolving motion called the golf swing, I, too, must focus on segments of it, for the sake of clarity. But please understand, it's a single entity. Once the movement begins, there's no stopping until you've finished the swing and the ball is on its way. That's because there's no place to stop, no seam where the pieces have been stitched together, no separate pages like the ones in this book, between which a marker will fit conveniently. The swing is like a single piece of fabric or a one-page document, and it begins with a hip turn.

"Turn in a Barrel"

In 1946, a golf professional with the unlikely name of Percy Boomer published a book entitled *On Learning Golf*. If you consider yourself a student of this game, that book should be in your library. It's a different type of instructional book because it focuses not on the mechanical aspects of the swing, but rather on how those mechanical aspects *feel*. On a first reading, you may find his anecdotal material a bit obscure, his syntax odd, his choice of words unusual. (He was English, you know.) But stick with it, because there are some real nuggets inside, and perhaps the most important is his description of the hip turn.

While trying to convey the sensation of the proper pivot, as he called it, Boomer asked a student to imagine that he was standing in a barrel that was hip-high. The top of the barrel was a snug fit, with enough clearance for the hips to rotate freely, but not move laterally. Once the student had that image in his mind, Boomer told him to turn his hips, keeping them on the same level as the top of the barrel. That is the best description of the correct lower-body action I've ever read. I can't improve on it and I'm not going to try.

Boomer also emphasized that the lower body is active while the upper body is passive. In other words, all movement is initiated with the hips, which is the cornerstone of my method. The hips *act* and the shoulders, arms, and hands *react*.

With that as preface, I'll briefly describe the takeaway I teach.

1. Holding the club lightly with your natural grip and addressing the ball as I described earlier, start the swing by turning your relaxed hips to the right in a smooth and deliberate manner. You want this turn to be stationary and level, as if you were turning in a barrel.

2. As a result of this hip turn, your relaxed and passive shoulders will turn, and you want them to remain level while turning, like the hips.

3. Your shoulders will cause your passive arms and hands to swing to the right.

4. As your hands move, they will drag the club back to the inside, like the rope and rock, following the path of the hips and shoulders.

5. With your hands approaching waist height, the club should begin to swing up into a vertical attitude and your wrists should start to hinge, or cock, into a concave, or cupped, position.

Having described the how, I'll now explain the why.

With a 5-iron, the ball is positioned slightly forward of center.

The lower body starts the takeaway.

Note the levelness of Paul Azinger's hip turn. His left knee will soon be pointing behind the ball.

Paul is relaxed at address.

A Level, Stationary Hip Turn

The hips should be turned level, because not only is that the most effective way to turn them for purposes of swinging a golf club, but it's also the most natural way to turn them. As I've said before, the more natural the movement, the easier it is to repeat. To turn them level, you should start from a position that feels much like you're sitting down.

By turning level, your hips also enjoy their greatest range of motion. When you cock them or tilt them, you restrict how far they can turn. As a consequence, you limit how far your *shoulders* can turn, and a limited shoulder turn means less power. Moreover, if your hip turn is restricted, you're more prone to activate your upper body, because you'll sense that your swing isn't going to be big enough. When that happens, you'll try to make it bigger by lifting the club with your hands and arms, or by trying to turn your shoulders against the resistance of your hips, or both. Either of these remedial maneuvers promotes hitting from

His arms and shoulders are reacting to the level turn of his hips.

From this position, Paul will "stand the club up" almost vertically.

the top or "casting" the club (like a fisherman casting a lure), a common problem with amateur golfers.

You get a similar result when your hips are tense, too. You want your hips to be relaxed so they'll turn easily and fully and allow your shoulders to do the same without strain. Another reason you want them relaxed is so you will be able to move them quickly.

Distance is a product of club-head speed squarely applied at impact. The quickness of your hip turn back to the ball, transmitted *to* the club head *through* your passive upper body, is what creates that club-head speed. You hit the ball farther by turning your hips quicker or faster, not by trying to hit harder with your hands and arms. Think of the hammer thrower at a track and field meet who spins faster to throw that ball and chain farther.

Your hip turn should be stationary because the shape of a centrifugal-force swing is circular. You're swinging around your spine, or, as some of my students like to think of it, around your center of gravity. Lateral movement alters the path of the club head and diminishes its speed.

At the risk of getting ahead of myself, let me also mention that a level hip is important because it helps establish the proper swing plane. With passive hands and arms, the club head tends to follow the lead of the hips and the club will be routed properly going back and up. However, if you cock or tilt your hips, the club won't go back on the correct plane without some compensating manipulation with your hands.

That's probably more about the lower body's role than you were expecting to see in a chapter on the takeaway. But after all, the takeaway is the first part of the swing itself. Starting back with the club correctly is essential. Believe me, I haven't been wasting your time.

A Relaxed, Level Shoulder Turn

A level hip turn also encourages a level shoulder turn, which is the most natural way for the shoulders to turn. A level shoulder

Standing the Club Up

As your hands approach waist height, your right arm should fold in against your side and you should swing the club up in a near-vertical attitude. Think of it as "standing the club up." As you'll notice, it requires little effort to hold the club that way. Standing the club up establishes an upright plane for your golfing pendulum, and it also helps produce the correct in-to-out swing path without hand or arm manipulation.

Turning your hips and shoulders level while swinging the club up may take some getting used to, especially if you've been

Stand the club up going back.

Don't "lay it off" like this. You're only adding unnecessary moves.

trying to swing the club and turn your shoulders on roughly the same plane, but it's a much easier way to play.

Swinging the club up in a vertical attitude with your lower body isn't the same thing as the early set I mentioned above. The early set is an active movement of the hands and wrists. This is passive. Also, if your upper body is passive, there's no need to try to keep your left arm straight when you swing the club up with your hips. The outward pull of centrifugal force on the club head will keep it straight enough.

A consequence of standing the club up on the takeaway, together with a natural grip, is that it encourages your wrists to cock or hinge into a concave or cupped position. I'll discuss this more fully in the chapter on the position at the top, our last fundamental. However, I thought I should at least mention it now, because if you've been a good student and have been practicing the takeaway already, you may have noticed it happening naturally.

Tempo, the Waggle, and the Forward Press

Another important objective of the takeaway is to set the rhythm or tempo of the swing.

Your takeaway should always be smooth and deliberate, even slow. The ball isn't going anywhere until you hit it, and you don't hit it with your backswing, so there's no reason to rush. A slow takeaway allows you time to coordinate all the components, and it greatly increases the chances that your club will arrive at the top "quietly."

Many golfers don't understand that the backswing, of which the takeaway is its first segment, is primarily a *positional move*, not a power-generating one. Good tempo certainly helps create club-head speed, and in that sense a slow takeaway contributes to generating power. However, you should think of the backswing as something you do to get to the proper position at the top and nothing more.

This isn't new advice either, not by a long shot. For instance, here's a quote from a delightful book I read recently entitled *Hints on the Game of Golf,* by Horace Hutchinson, a two-time winner of the British Amateur championship. Published in 1886, it was the first book of golf instruction and a best-seller in its day.

> I would not like to say it is impossible to raise the club too slowly, but certainly the danger is all the other way. Golfers have gone so far as to instruct their caddies to say to them, "Slow back," so as to keep them in mind of this precept each time they addressed themselves to drive the ball. "Slow back!"—it is a valuable text to have at heart. Some write it up in their dressingrooms and read it every morning all the while they shave.

"Slow back"—still great advice. The next time someone tells you that the only good instruction is the latest instruction, remember Mr. Hutchinson's book. The only thing I would change about that quote is the first sentence. If I had written it, it would read: "It's impossible to *swing* the club back *with your lower body too slowly.*"

Fast takeaways are usually hand-activated. If that's the case, then you're not swinging the club back with your lower body, but raising it with your upper body. If your takeaway has been a hands-and-arms affair, a hip-initiated takeaway may seem ponderously slow at first because the lower body, although much stronger, is slower than the upper body. However, keep practicing until it becomes instinctive. The effort will pay big dividends later, especially when you're under pressure and have to hit a good shot.

To help you start back smoothly and deliberately, there are a couple of devices you can use when playing. In terms of their position in the overall sequence of things, they actually occur before the takeaway begins. For purposes of presentation, however, I reversed the order, thinking that would be more beneficial. I've heard them referred to as "swing antifreeze," and that's a good way of thinking about them. The first is the waggle.

To the uninitiated, the waggle might look like vacillation in the midst of an anxiety attack. The golfer looks back and forth, from the target to the ball, then back to the target. He twists his shoulders and hips. He bounces his feet. He breaks the club back with his hands, then waves the club head around behind the ball. With some players, it can go on for quite a while.

By waggling, however, the better golfer is trying to sense the swing before he makes it. Think of it as a swing in miniature or an abbreviated dress rehearsal before the big performance. He's visualizing the direction and trajectory of the shot that he needs to hit, he's alerting his muscles that they'll soon be called into action, and he's reminding them of their role and order of participation. He's establishing the tempo of the forthcoming swing, too.

Tommy Armour was fond of an old Scottish saying: "As ye waggle, so shall ye swing." He could tell a great deal about a player by watching him waggle. A quick, jerky waggle meant a fast, fitful swing, while a smooth, deliberate waggle usually evolved into a flowing takeaway and a good, rhythmic swing.

However, a more prosaic, though no less important, purpose of the waggle for the accomplished golfer is to keep his muscles relaxed and in motion. And that brings us to our second device—the forward press.

The forward press is a small, pre-swing movement that breaks the adhesions, you might say. It's a little motion that starts the big motion. The most common type of forward press is a small twist of the hips to the left and a slight press of the hands forward, before the hips turn back to the right, starting the takeaway. Its role is more limited than the waggle, and while almost all of the better golfers use a waggle, some don't use a forward press. The ones who don't usually continue to waggle until the last possible instant. One way or the other, the good player wants to be in motion as he starts his swing. A big reason for that is Sir Isaac Newton's First Law of Motion, or, as it's more commonly known, the law of inertia.

A simplified version of the great scientist's law might read:

A body at rest tends to stay at rest and a body in motion tends to continue in motion unless acted upon by something else.

Inertia is the reason why the first few yards of a footrace are the slowest and why it takes more effort to get a heavy object rolling than to keep it rolling. The object's mass is working against you rather than for you. Perhaps, like me, you drove an old clunker as a teenager and let the battery run down, then had to start it by pushing it. Remember how hard it was to get it moving? However, after the old car was rolling, it wasn't nearly as difficult to keep it rolling. That's inertia.

Inertia has its part to play in golf, as well. Now, a golf club isn't as heavy as an old car, and neither are you, but if you start the swing correctly, the momentum you and the club develop will help you continue correctly. Start it incorrectly, however, and you're swimming against the tide, so to speak, not with it. And it's difficult to consistently start the club back correctly from a dead stop. That's why the waggle and the forward press can be so helpful.

Using either, or maybe both, you keep your muscles relaxed and yourself in motion. You've overcome inertia before the start of the swing. Otherwise, your takeaway may be more like a nervous spasm or jerk, rather than the smooth, deliberate, and flowing motion that it should be.

Summary

The takeaway begins with a level and stationary turn of your hips to the right. Your lower body should be relaxed so that your hips will turn easily and fully.

Your shoulders will follow naturally, also turning level, and causing your arms to swing. Your upper body should be passive and just as relaxed as your lower body, if not more, so that it will react to what the lower body is doing.

If you have a light grip, the club head will lag slightly behind the hands as they start back. As your hands approach waist height, the club should begin to swing up into a vertical attitude with your wrists starting to cock into a cupped position.

The takeaway should be a smooth and deliberate movement. Remember Horace Hutchinson's advice—slow back! A waggle and/or a forward press will help you stay in motion at address so you're not starting from a dead stop.

There's an excellent warm-up exercise that will help you become familiar with the sensations of level hip and shoulder turns. Place a club under your buttocks, lean forward slightly with your back straight, and turn your hips from side to side with your shoulders following.

APPLICATION

*"It should feel like you're dragging the club
to the top."*

Several months ago, a Hollywood executive came to me for help.
He was suffering through a spell of golf's most devastating
afflictions—the shanks. Most players don't even like to hear the
word. (About the only thing which can equal it for sheer demor-
alization is yipping short putts.) If you're one of the fortunate
few who have never hit one and don't know what it is, a shank
is what happens when you strike the ball with the hosel or neck
of an iron rather than with its face.

I asked this executive if he was hitting a closed-face or open-
face shank. He gave me a funny look and said, "I don't know.
What's the difference?"

A closed-face shank usually occurs when you fall forward
onto your toes as you swing down, so that at impact the
clubhead is farther away from your feet than it was at address.
An open-face shank happens when the blade is open in the impact area and the club's hosel reaches the ball first. However,
rather than explain all that to him, I simply asked him to hit a
few shots. As it turned out, his was an open-face shank and the
problem started with his takeaway.

His first move was an exaggerated forward press with his
hands which pre-cocked his wrists and opened the club face.
Then he swung the club back inside abruptly, thrusting the club
head around behind him. That left him in a flat, laid-off position
at the top and from there, a simple turn through the ball coming
down will not square the blade at impact.

A player with fast hands can sometimes rescue such a swing
by actively rotating his forearms. (But the timing must be near-

perfect. If he over-rotates, he'll hit a duck hook. If he under-rotates, he'll block the shot.) My new student, however, didn't have fast hands. To compound the problem, he was sliding laterally on the downswing which left the club face open even more at impact. Occasionally, he would manage to hit one straight (more or less), but most of his shots were either big blocks or cold shanks off the hosel. It was not a pretty sight.

"It starts with your takeaway," I told him. "The club must go back square. You're fanning it open. And you can't take it back inside right away, either. Here's what I want you to try.

"Start the takeaway with your lower body and just leave the club head on the ground. Imagine that you're holding one end of a rope and there's a rock tied to the other end. I want you to drag the rock back by turning your lower body."

He took a practice swing and gave me one of those this-isn't-going-to-work looks. "It feels like I'm going to shank it even more!" he said.

"Try it anyway."

Well, he did and for the first time in a while he caught the ball squarely on the face of the club. He stood there for a moment with this surprised look on his face. Then he raked another range ball from the pile, took his stance and hit it flush, too.

"Am I doing this right?" he asked, as if those two might have been flukes.

"Don't change a thing."

He hit several more and it got better and better. Then, perhaps caught up in the moment, he lapsed back to his old takeaway and clanked one off the hosel again.

"What happened?" he asked. "I took the club back the right way, didn't I?"

"No, you didn't."

"Well, it felt like I did."

"Maybe it felt that way for an inch or two, but you need to keep that same feeling all the way up. It should feel like you're dragging the club back all the way to the top. Then, on the downswing, it should feel like you're dragging the club down to the ball, too."

Retaining the sensation of the lag takeaway throughout the swing is an excellent way to keep your hands passive and the club face square. Once my new student got the hang of it, he started to hit the ball solid. That afternoon, he played with a touring pro friend of his who had witnessed his shanks the day before.

Afterwards, the pro told me, "John, I don't know what you showed him, but he didn't hit one of those 'funny shots' all day."

I had to laugh. He wouldn't even say the word.

In 1944, Bob Hamilton defeated Byron Nelson to win the PGA Championship. Bob was from Evansville, Indiana, just across the Ohio River from my hometown of Henderson, Kentucky, and as a teenager, I spent many, many hours at his driving range.

He was a marvelous wedge player, one of the finest I have ever seen. I would watch him, then try to imitate him. To this day, I still have a vivid mental image of him hitting wedges. He had learned from the legendary hustler Titanic Thompson and, like Titanic, Bob could hit them from either side, right-handed or left-handed.

He was a big believer in turning the lower body and turning it level. He was also a big believer in passive hands. It was most evident in his takeaway.

Bob always took the club back in one piece. His club head, hands, arms and shoulders all moved away from the ball together, propelled by the turn of his hips. (By the way, that's exactly the way Sam Snead takes the club back, too.) And while I never saw Bob use a pronounced lag of the club head, like Bobby Jones and Tommy Armour did with their old wooden-shafted clubs, I often saw the hint of a lag because of his passive hands.

It doesn't have to be a big production. All you're trying to do is capture the sensation of dragging the club head back and that doesn't take much. I take the club back that way all the time and very few people ever notice the lag. What they do notice, however, is how squarely I strike the ball, and it all starts with the takeaway.

THE POSITION
AT THE TOP

Now we approach what is arguably the most important moment in the swing—the change of direction at the top. Of course, the shot lives or dies by what happens at impact, but if you handle this transition correctly, then good, square impact is almost automatic.

As I related earlier, the backswing begins with a level and stationary turn of the hips. If you are to reach the proper position at the top, your hip turn should be a full, unrestricted one. Your lower body must be relaxed, almost loose, so that your hips will turn easily.

Think about turning your hips so that your left rear pants pocket faces the target on the backswing and your right front pants pocket faces the target on the downswing. You might imagine them as a well-oiled flywheel mounted horizontally, or you could envision yourself sitting in a chair with rollers on the bottom and swiveling around. If you're still having trouble, then try that dance from the early 1960s called the Twist. That should loosen them up.

There are only two limitations on the extent of your hip turn, and they both pertain to your right knee. First, keep your right knee positioned inside of or directly over the right ankle. Never allow it to bow out. Second, always maintain some flex in your right knee. Don't let it stiffen up. Even with these two restrictions, however, you should still be able to turn your hips about 45 degrees without any strain, and that's ample for the purpose of hitting a golf ball.

As your hips turn, so will your shoulders, but remember, their role is a passive one. Your shoulders should never do anything independently of the hips. The hips act and the shoulders react. Earlier, I said that the shoulders, like the hips, turn level. Let me explain what I mean by a *level* shoulder turn.

Viewed from the side, it's readily apparent that when addressing the ball, a golfer tilts his spine as he bends forward from the waist. With that in mind, does "level" mean that he turns his shoulders level with (parallel to) the ground or level with (perpendicular to) his spine? Or is it level in terms of something else?

I want you to turn your shoulders so they feel level or parallel to the ground.

Now, I didn't say turn them so that they *are* level, only so that they *feel* level to the ground. There's a difference. One way to think about it is to turn your left shoulder "up" to your chin. Another, for those of you who are right-side-oriented, is to turn so that your right shoulder feels low at the top of the backswing. (I'm talking about a small movement here, so if you feel any strain or discomfort keeping your right shoulder low at the top, then you're overdoing it.) A third swing thought that has been helpful to some of my students is to think about turning around and shaking hands with someone directly behind you, without moving your feet.

There are several reasons why I recommend a shoulder turn that feels level with the ground. First, it promotes a deeper and thus more powerful turn. Notice how the big muscles across your back seem to come alive when you turn level. They're ready to go to work, but in a passive or reactive way.

Second, it allows you to turn your body behind the ball.

To make a level shoulder turn, think about turning to shake hands with someone directly behind you.

From that position, it's much easier to deliver the club face squarely into the back of the ball at impact.

Third, a shoulder turn that feels level with the ground is insurance against dipping or dropping your *left* shoulder as you swing the club back. A low left shoulder at the top, where you've turned your left shoulder *under* your chin, encourages a weak, shallow turn. All that your hands and arms can do from that position is lift the club steeply on the backswing, then drop it abruptly on the ball on the downswing. Basically, a low left shoulder robs you of power because it takes the hips and shoulders out of action. If you'll pardon an old military analogy, it's as if the enemy has spiked your cannons. No golfer of championship caliber, at least none that I know of, has ever played with a dipped left shoulder.

One more thought about the way your torso or trunk turns before we proceed to the arms and hands. *Never turn your shoulders independently of your hips.* The length of your backswing is determined by your hip turn. To swing long, you must turn long with the hips. You don't swing long by turning your shoulders against the resistance of your hips. There's no need to. If you're a reasonably limber person, a hip turn of 45 degrees will usually produce about a 90-degree shoulder turn, creating a big arc with plenty of room to generate club-head speed.

With your shoulders turning level, your arms will naturally follow, swinging back passively. Because of your light grip, the club head may drag a little as it starts back, but it will soon catch up with the hands and reestablish that straight line from the left shoulder to the club head. Then, as your hands approach waist height, the club should begin to swing up vertically with your left wrist hinging into a cupped position. The club head should also swing up outside the hands. At this point, everything has been set in motion and you merely allow it to continue to the top.

So, it's a level hip turn, a level shoulder turn with your arms swinging back, the club standing up and your wrists starting to cock into a cupped position. And remember—slow back! Keep it smooth and deliberate. The backswing is primarily a positional move, not a power-generating move.

As the club swings higher, its weight will cause your left wrist to cock even more. The cupped position is the most natural way for your wrist to cock and, in my opinion, it's the best position at the top from which to play. Let me demonstrate why.

Lay your left hand and forearm flat on a table with the palm down. Without moving your forearm, raise your hand so that it folds back toward your wrist. Notice how far the back of your hand moves.

Most people can easily raise their hand over 60 degrees. I have a touch of arthritis in my hands and wrists and I can still raise mine about 75 degrees. With my young students, it's almost 90. This movement is called "dorsal flexion," and you can see the range of motion is substantial.

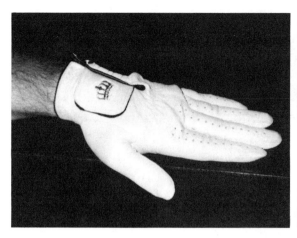 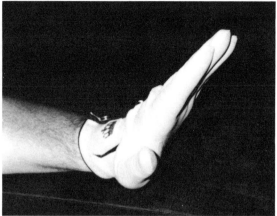

The "cupped" position is the most natural way to cock your left wrist and provides a greater range of motion.

Now, another demonstration. Again, lay your left forearm and hand flat on the table with your palm down. But this time I want you to move your hand to the left without lifting it, while keeping your wrist still.

This movement is called "radial deviation," and you may recognize it as a commonly recommended way of cocking your left

With the "flat" position, the range of motion is significantly less.

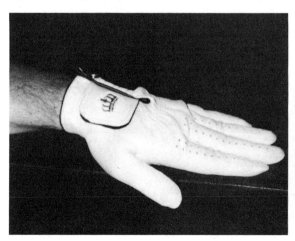 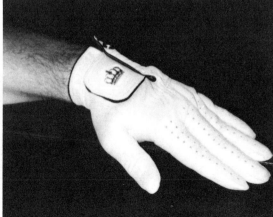

wrist at the top. If you're like most people, the range of motion this way is significantly less, maybe only 25 degrees.

This comparison is important, because the more your left wrist cocks, the more club-head speed you can generate. Not only does the cupped position allow you to cock your wrist more, it also feels more comfortable, more natural. There's no strain on your wrists and thus you're less likely to hit from the top.

In addition to the cupped and flat positions, there's a third way to cock your wrists. It's called the arched position (or "palmar flexion" if you want the technical name) and I mention it here only to say *don't use it.* Of the three, it's far and away the most difficult position to play from and in all my years of golf, I've only seen a handful of top-caliber players who've used it. You must be as strong as the village blacksmith to play well with an arched left wrist because you'll spend your golfing life trying to "block" the ball on line at the target and not hit duck hooks. Trust me. It's much easier to play with a cupped, or even a flat, left wrist.

The "cupped" position is the best way to cock your left wrist.
The "arched" position is the worst.

To feel how the wrists should cock naturally, assume your address position and raise the club without lifting your arms.

Here's another demonstration of how to cock your wrists naturally. First assume your address position, then raise the club shaft toward your chin without lifting your arms.

From this position, it's very simple to get to the proper position at the top. Just turn your torso and raise your arms.

The combination of a natural grip and this cupped left wrist gives you the best of both worlds. Your hips and shoulders turn level, which is the most natural and effective way for them to turn, while the club swings on an upright plane. With an upright swing plane and passive hands, the club face remains square to the target longer through the impact area, increasing the chances for solid contact and a straight shot. And it's accomplished without any forearm rotation, a maneuver which is difficult to time and only complicates the swing.

The correct position at the top of the backswing.

At the top, this is the position you're looking for. I'll describe it starting from the ground up (which, incidentally, is the way the swing should start).

The right knee is flexed, and it's either directly over the ankle or just inside of it. The left heel is slightly off the ground, and the left knee is pointing in behind the ball. The hips have turned fully, with the left rear pants pocket facing the target. This hip turn is level and stationary.

Responding to the hips, the shoulders have also turned level, meaning that they feel level in relation to the ground. If you're a limber and flexible person, your back may face the target. If you're not, don't worry about it. Just turn as far as you can without discomfort or strain.

Responding to the shoulders, the arms have swung the club back and then up on a rather steep plane. At the top, the cupped left wrist is directly under the shaft and the weight of the club rests on the left thumb. The knuckles of the right hand are pointing straight up, not "laid off" behind in what some call the tray position. The right elbow has remained close to the side.

Whether the club reaches a horizontal position at the top is unimportant. Remember—the length of the backswing is determined by the hip turn. A bigger club-head arc is nice to have, but not at the expense of doing something that will encourage hitting from the top, like lifting the club with your arms or straining to turn your shoulders against the resistance of your hips. That's being penny-wise and pound-foolish, as an aunt of mine used to say.

I'm not concerned with whether the club shaft "crosses the line" a little either. That's a checkpoint used by those instructors who teach "hand-and-arm-active" swings. Besides, most good golfers cross the line anyway.

Do You Really Pause at the Top?

We've all heard the expression "the pause at the top," and perhaps you thought there was a real pause, when everything comes to a complete halt. You're not alone. Many golfers think that everything does stop, and I'm sure the belief has been reinforced with the use of video cameras, as I've mentioned before. It probably started as helpful advice for someone with a fast swing. But let me set the record straight—there is no pause at the top, at least not in the sense that *everything* just stops. What might appear to be a complete pause is really an illusion, something like a magician's trick, a golfing sleight of hand (actually, sleight of hips is more accurate).

You're familiar with how magicians do it, aren't you? They divert your attention. You look at one hand while they're doing the trick with the other. Something like that happens during the golf swing.

Watch an accomplished golfer like Paul Azinger. As his club changes direction from backswing to downswing, the upper half of his body does appear to stop momentarily. It's much the same as when a golf ball is tossed into the air. The ball goes up, then as it reaches its highest point, it appears to hover for an instant before falling. But the upper body isn't the whole story.

Think of a duck swimming across a pond. On the surface, the duck glides along, appearing almost motionless. However, underneath the water, its webbed feet are paddling away. In a sense, that's what is happening with the golf swing, because *the hips never stop moving.* Once you've turned your hips to the right as far as they'll go, you immediately turn them back to the left. That's why I say that the pause at the top is an illusion. The club may stop momentarily, and so may your arms and shoulders. But things are still moving down below.

Actually, I would encourage you to think in terms of the upper body pausing. Just swing the club up, then leave it there and walk out from under it, so to speak. That will help the club arrive quietly at the top, and it will help keep your hands passive.

So, turn your hips to the right and the upper body follows, swinging the club up in a vertical attitude. Your wrists will begin to cock into a cupped position, and as the club nears its apex, its weight and momentum will cause your wrists to cock even more. Then your hips, having completed their turn to the right, reverse direction and turn back to the left. *Because your upper body started back after your lower body and because it has farther to go anyway, it should still be moving up (or have just arrived at the top) when the hips have started back down.*

This instant of opposition, when the upper body is going in one direction while the lower body has reversed itself and started in the other, completes the cocking of your wrists. It also helps preserve this wrist cock well into the downswing. It's an excellent way of making the swing simple and adding power at the same time. It works especially well under pressure.

I said in an earlier chapter that the takeaway was one of the two places where your hands were the most likely to become active and that you can prevent it by swinging the club back with your hips. The other place where the hands are most likely to try to take control of the swing is at the top, when the club changes directions. A real pause at the top—and by that I mean *everything* comes to a halt—is an invitation for your hands to take charge on the way down. You prevent that by keeping your grip light and your hips moving. If you start your hips down while your hands are still going up, then the hands won't have the opportunity to take over.

Constantly moving your hips also keeps your swing compact by not allowing your arms the time to lift the club on the backswing. Many of my students, and Paul is one of them, don't take the club back to horizontal at the top. However, they do make a full shoulder turn because they make a full hip turn. An overly long swing, in which the club dips past horizontal, usually means the golfer's hands are in control and he's trying to squeeze something extra out of the swing by lifting the club. Often the only thing extra he gets is misery.

Lifting the club may cause it to rebound or bounce at the top. Invariably, it will bounce out and over the shot, producing a pull or pulled slice. The same thing can happen if your backswing is fast, because fast backswings are usually caused by anxious, active hands. Even when the club doesn't bounce, you're inclined to hit from the top or unload early. But if your hips are in control and in constant motion, and the club arrives quietly at the top, your backswing will be compact and your hands more likely to remain passive. Also, your wrists will remain cocked until well into the downswing, where your light grip will allow the club head to release itself.

Speaking of keeping the wrists cocked well into the downswing, there are some excellent players, like Lee Trevino, for example, who don't cock their wrists *until* the downswing. Think of it as insurance against hitting from the top. You can only cock and uncock your wrists once during the swing. If you unload early, you won't have time to cock them a second time. To prevent a premature uncocking, Trevino stands the club up on the backswing and then cocks his wrists with the motion of his hips as he turns back to the ball. His wrists both cock and uncock on the downswing. It's not a technique for everybody, but it's something you may want to experiment with on the practice tee.

As I mentioned before, starting down with the hips while the club is still swinging up is an excellent way to generate more power. It creates an instant of tautness or tension, with the upper and lower body moving in different directions, which greatly increases club-head speed. However, this tautness is generated and released so quickly (released by the hips, I might add) that there's no chance of its causing you to hit from the top.

Another piece of sage advice, this one as old as the hills, is to *return the right elbow to your side* on the way down. That will help establish the proper downswing path. You might even want to think in terms of the right elbow leading the right forearm down to make sure your hands and the club come down last.

A Redistribution of Weight

I don't teach a lateral slide with the lower body, and I don't like the term "weight shift." If I told ten new students to shift their weight, nine of them would lean to the right, resting momentarily on one foot, then lean back to the left. They would look like trees in the wind, and in the process their heads and spines might move twelve inches or more. That's enough to ruin a centrifugal-force swing.

If I told the same ten to make a lateral slide with their lower bodies to start the downswing, they would hold their heads back while moving their hips to the left. In the process, all would drop the right shoulder. When you drop the right shoulder on the downswing, you alter both the path of the club head and the alignment of the club face. If you don't hit the shot fat, you will generally hit a push that flies to the right of the target. Do that a few times and instinctively you'll try to correct for the altered alignment by rotating your forearms or twisting your shoulders open to change the downswing path of the club.

I understand why many instructors tell their students to make a weight shift or a lateral slide to start the downswing—it's to keep them from hitting the ball with their weight on their right side. There are several variations. In one, the golfer simply "hangs back," meaning he either puts most of his weight on his right foot at address or shifts it there on the backswing, then leaves it there during the downswing.

A second variation is the "reverse weight shift"—the golfer leans forward on the backswing, then leans back on the forward swing, so to speak. A third is the "spinout"—the golfer starts the downswing by spinning his hips to the left, but his weight remains on his right side.

The consequences of these are much the same. With the golfer's weight primarily on his right side, the hips never clear out of the way, so the hands and arms can't swing the club down and in on its proper path, but rather must go out and over. The club head descends on the ball rather steeply from outside the intended line, and the result is a pull or a pull slice, depending on the alignment of the club face. Seldom is there any sting in the shot, because the golfer is leaning away from what he's trying to hit, much like a boxer who leans away from his opponent when he delivers a punch. Not much chance of a knockout there. Also, golfers who swing with their weight on the back foot usually unload early or throw the club from the top with their hands. They're easy to recognize. They're the ones who are off-balance and falling back as they swing.

The weight shift and the lateral slide are intended as remedies for these problems. However, while they help in some cases, they cause problems in others, much like a medicine with strong side effects. If you're hitting off your back foot, Dr. Redman prescribes "turning in the barrel" and letting your own momentum take care of the situation. If that isn't specific enough, I'll repeat three things I mentioned earlier.

First, to get the sensations of a correct turn, use the warm-up drill of placing a club under your buttocks, then turning your hips and shoulders. Second, think of turning your hips so that your left rear pants pocket faces the target on the backswing and your right front pants pocket faces the target on the follow-through. Third, hold the club securely, but lightly, so that the hands will remain passive. In my opinion, many golfers who hit off their back foot do so not only because they don't turn their torsos enough, but because their hands are active leaders, not passive followers.

Is there a redistribution of weight during the swing? Yes, absolutely. But it should be the result of your turn, not something you deliberately try to make happen by leaning laterally or pushing off one foot or the other.

I've read that the arm of an average-sized man weighs between ten and twelve pounds. If you extend both of your arms to the right, you add twenty or more pounds to the weight your right foot is supporting. Imagine the momentum you generate by simply turning your hips and swinging your arms. It's no wonder that a golfer who knows how to apply that momentum can hit a little golf ball a long way.

Just hold the club lightly, turn your hips fully (as you did with the warm-up drill), and let your arms swing, directing the momentum through the ball and toward the target. Then allow that same momentum to pull you over to your left side. Your weight will shift, but it's not something you do intentionally; it just happens.

Club-Head Release

Now we arrive at the swing's moment of truth. Frankly, all that has gone before is simply preparation for this instant. Yet, in writing about it, it seems almost anticlimactic. That's probably because after the hips have reversed their direction and initiated the downswing, the remainder of the swing is essentially a reflexive action. However, there's nothing anticlimactic about watching a skillful player strike the ball crisply or experiencing the sensations of a squarely hit shot yourself. It's a prime reason why this ancient game is thriving still.

Passive hands and arms are the key to a proper release because they let the outward pull of centrifugal force and the club head's momentum uncock your wrists at the optimum instant.

I think it would be instructive to begin this section with a few photographs.

Please pay particular attention to the angle between Paul's left forearm and the club shaft. In the first two pictures on page 93, the angle is between 80 and 90 degrees. In the third, it's increased to about 120 degrees. And in the fourth, it's opened to 180 degrees, reestablishing the straight line that the club shaft and his left arm formed at address.

This is photographic evidence of what some have called the secret of golf. It's also been referred to as hitting late, the delayed hit, the late uncocking of the wrists, and clubhead lag, among other terms. It's a major reason why wiry little 145-pound guys can hit 290-yard drives and make it look easy. Unfortunately, what these photographs can't show you is how it feels.

To the skilled amateur and the professional, swinging the club and striking the ball with this action is almost as automatic as breathing. To the on-again, off-again weekend golfer, it's elusive. When he has it, golf is euphoric child's play, but it's a miserable and frustrating waste of time when he doesn't. To the high-handicapper, someone who's never experienced it at all, it's like magic. Yet, this secret is no secret at all.

All you do is *let centrifugal force and the momentum of the club head uncock your wrists*. That's it. There's no sorcery involved, no mystical incantation under a full moon. Just hold the club passively, keep your wrists relaxed so they work like hinges, then allow centrifugal force to open those hinges.

There are two problems, however. First, we all have a strong, instinctive urge to use our hands, no matter what we're doing. And why not? They're right there at the ends of our arms and we can do so many things with them. Their role in the golf swing is certainly an important one, because with them we hold the tool that we use to strike the ball. But most golfers not only overuse them, but use them incorrectly, because common sense tells them to.

When a beginner first picks up a club and tries to hit a golf ball, invariably he will exert pressure on the *side* of the shaft with his hands. Ask him why and you'll certainly get a puzzled expression and maybe a reply like "How else am I going to hit it if I don't?"

Common sense tells you that in order to hit the ball, you must manipulate the club head by putting pressure on the shaft. Unfortunately, this is one of those times when common sense is dead wrong. When you manipulate the club head you are manually uncocking your wrists, forcing open the angle between the left forearm and the club shaft with hand and arm pressure, and not giving centrifugal force and the momentum of the club head the opportunity to do it. Unless you are one in a million, you will never be able to do it as powerfully, as accurately, or as dependably as they can. As Ernest Jones said, trying to use the club like a lever is the greatest obstacle to swinging correctly.

We human beings find it difficult to trust things we can't see. We can feel centrifugal force and club-head momentum working, and we can even see their effects, but we can't actually see

An example of how *not* to do it. Hitting from the top is the result when you "push" on the shaft to make the club head move.

them. So you have to learn to trust them. You do that by giving them a chance on the practice tee, where mis-hit shots are no big deal. Then, once you are confident they will work and work dependably, you can take them onto the course and amaze your buddies.

To help you work through these problems, I've collected a few swing thoughts. Remember, the goal is to preserve your wrist cock until the bottom of the downswing, where centrifugal force and the increasing momentum of the swinging club head will uncock your wrists and slam the club face into the back of the ball. And what should your hands do, other than hold the club lightly? Nothing.

1. *Leave the club at the top and walk out from under it.* This is one of my favorites, because it captures the essence of a completely passive upper body. You swing the club up and you leave it there as you start the downswing with your lower body. Obviously, the club won't remain up there long. But the point is that your hands and arms will remain passive, moving only in response to the hips.

2. *Swing a rope and a rock.* Another favorite. Imagine the club as a rope with a rock tied to the end.

3. *Toll the bell.* This is an old one. I've included it because the image involves a rope. To toll the bell, obviously you must pull down on the bell rope, and a rope, being flexible, isn't something you can use as a lever. Or, as I've heard many times, you can pull a rope, but you can't push it. The problem with this is it might encourage you to start the downswing by pulling down with your arms. If tolling the bell happens in response to a hip turn, then use it with my blessings.

4. *Keep the hands in front of the club head as long as possible.* This was a favorite of Tommy Armour. My reservation with it is that it focuses attention on the hands and not the hips, where it should be. However, it can be helpful if your hands remain passive and your grip light.

Keep your hands ahead of the club head.

5. *Think tug-of-war.* This one tries to capture the sensation of pulling the club through the hitting area once it's approximately parallel to the ground.

All of these swing thoughts encourage a pulling action, and the good swing is a pulling action produced by the lower body. Also, when the club is pulled down, the club head is the last thing in line to move. The result is a release that feels like cracking a whip.

If you're someone who plays by throwing the club from the top, you're probably wondering, "But if I don't put pressure on the side of the shaft, how will the club head ever catch up with the hands at impact?"

Good question.

It's usually answered in terms of hitting against a firm left side or, in other words, stiffening your left leg as your hands approach the hitting area. When you do that, you set off a chain reaction of resistance that works up through the body, eventually slowing the hands and allowing the club head to catch up. (The late Tony Lema even tried to stop his hands as they approached the hitting area in order to add to this whiplash effect.)

As an explanation, hitting against a firm left side is fine, as far as it goes, because your hands, arms, and torso do slow down slightly just before impact. It doesn't go far enough, however.

If you ever get the chance, watch my student Maggie Will play. A multiple winner on the LPGA Tour, Maggie is a little wisp of a lady who weighs only ninety-eight pounds, yet routinely drives the ball 250 yards. Pound for pound, she's the longest hitter I've ever seen, and she may be the longest on earth. Watch her nail a few drives and common sense will tell you that Maggie's doing something more than simply resisting with her lower body to slow her hands so the club head can catch up.

A technically complete answer is well beyond the scope of this book, and I'm sure that most readers wouldn't be interested in the details. But the club head really catches up because of centrifugal force and something else called the conservation of angular momentum. In a nutshell, here's how they work.

Centrifugal force is the outward pull on a rotating object. In a golf swing, when you turn your body and swing the club, you generate centrifugal force. You feel it more in your hands and arms because they have less mass than other parts of your body. However, the outward pull feels strongest on the club, because it's even lighter than your hands and arms. So, centrifugal force acts to pull the club head away from you, thus uncocking your wrists. The faster you turn, the more centrifugal force you generate and the stronger the outward pull, and you're turning the fastest just before impact.

The conservation of angular momentum is a principle of physics that deals with a force generated by a rotating object called (logically enough) angular momentum. When you turn your body to hit a golf ball, you create angular momentum. If your hands and arms remain passive, it will flow outward from your body, unrestricted, and upon reaching the club head, it will make the club head move very fast.

Something similar happens when a bullwhip cracks. The sound you hear is actually its tip breaking the sound barrier. To generate that much speed, the teamster or cattle driver (or whoever) creates momentum by using the big muscles of his back and shoulder to "throw" the whip's heavy handle. This momentum is transmitted down the length of the rolling lash. When it reaches the lagging tip, the tip speeds up because it's so much smaller and lighter than the whip's handle.

In comparing this phenomenon to the golf swing, a good illustration is that of a spinning ice skater. When a skater wants to spin very fast, she pulls her arms in against her body. When she wants to slow down, she does the opposite, extending them outward, and her rotational velocity slows instantly. This happens because when she extends her arms, she redistributes some of her momentum, which was concentrated in a small circle when her arms were pulled in, over a larger circle.

An accomplished golfer does much the same thing. At the top of his backswing, he's in a rather tight coil, much like the skater. Then he starts down by turning his hips back toward the target. He can move quickly at first because he is coiled. However, as his arms and the club swing away from his body, his rotational velocity slows slightly. That's because, according to the principle of the conservation of angular momentum, the momentum that he initially generated must now be redistributed over a wider area. So some of this big-muscle momentum is transmitted outward to the much smaller and lighter club head. The result is twofold—his hands, arms, and torso are slowing slightly while the club head is speeding up, and just in time to give the ball a real jolt.

What happens when you deliberately try to hit with your hands and arms? You interfere with the flow of this momentum and actually slow down the club head. I have read books and magazine articles in which teaching and playing professionals alike have advocated hitting late with the right hand or snapping the wrists through the ball at impact, implying that you should actively *push* on the club shaft with your hands. I disagree. Assuming that they are knowledgeable individuals, I'm sure they were describing the feeling of a result and not a cause.

I say that because in a centrifugal-force swing, you don't have time at the bottom of the downswing arc to deliberately hit with the right hand or snap your wrists. It's over with in a flash. Sure, the wrists snap, but you're not making them snap—the club head snaps because it's releasing like a whip. All you can do is hold on. And you're not hitting with the right hand, either. What you're feeling is the uncocking of your wrists by centrifugal force and by the accelerating club head being propelled by the body's outward-flowing momentum (according to the principle of the conservation of angular momentum).

A light, passive grip encourages a pulling action which retains power.

When the right hand puts pressure on the side of the shaft, the result is a scoop. There's no power here.

There's so much that can go wrong when you try to hit late with the right hand, even if you're a talented athlete. Most players, amateurs and professionals alike, will usually unload early when they try it. When that happens, they find themselves in the hitting area with nothing to hit with. I promise that you'll be a much better player if you stop trying to push the club down with your hands and learn to pull it down with your hips.

Here's something that should help. In the sequence of photographs on pages 100–101, in which I'm holding the club only with my right hand for the purpose of clear illustration, please note how I've cocked my wrist and maintained it through impact.

I'm not deliberately trying to hold that position, I've just gripped the club lightly and done nothing to disrupt it. By doing this, I've retained power until impact.

However, if I had tried to hit the ball by putting pressure on the side of the shaft with my hand (in other words, by using leverage), the result would have been a weak scoop.

Impact

Nowhere are the consequences of an active lower body and a passive upper body more evident than at impact. Take a look at the following photograph.

Paul's active hips have *turned,* generating the centrifugal force and momentum that power the swing, and *cleared,* opening a downswing path for the arms. His passive shoulders have followed and at impact are roughly parallel to the target line, just as they were at address. If he'd used his upper body actively, his shoulders would be open to the target and he would be out and over the shot.

His passive arms have been pulled down by the turning hips. The club swings down, butt first, until deep into the downswing arc, where the increasing outward pull of centrifugal force and a rush of momentum from his body to the club uncock his passive wrists with a snap and slam the club head squarely into the back

You achieve the correct position at impact by pulling passive shoulders, arms, and hands through the hitting area with active legs and hips.

By eliminating forearm rotation, you keep the club face on-line longer.

of the ball. That same momentum has propelled him toward his left side, where his weight will settle at the finish.

It is only after the ball is on its way and his left arm is folding in against his left side that his forearms will begin to rotate. Until that point in the swing, the only thing that's rotated has been his body.

To prove the point, take a look at these photographs of me hitting a wedge.

If I had rolled my hands and arms over through impact, the toe of my club would be pointing toward the sky in the second one. Obviously, I didn't and it hasn't. Looks like you could set a full drinking glass on the face of my wedge, doesn't it? By eliminating all hand manipulation and forearm rotation, you keep

Rotate your body, not your forearms.

the club face on-line longer and give yourself a better chance of hitting the ball at the target.

So, rotate your body, not your forearms.

Summary

The swing is a seamless whole that starts with a level, relaxed, and full hip turn. This turn is a stationary one, in the sense that there is no lateral movement or sway. The relaxed upper body follows, with the shoulders also turning level and the club swinging back and up in a vertical attitude. As the club nears its apex, the weight of the club head begins to cock the left wrist into a concave or cupped position.

Your hips, which started first and have completed their turn to the right, now turn back to the left with the upper body and the club still moving up. This instant of opposition, with the lower body and upper body moving in different directions, completes the wrist cock, which is retained well into the downswing, where a light grip allows the club head to release squarely into the ball. Then, with the ball on its way, the momentum of your turning body and swinging arms pulls you onto your left side.

APPLICATION

"The best little player in the world."

Maggie Will came to me in 1990 after struggling for a time. She was mis-hitting the ball—one shot would fly right, the next one left—and that's no way to make a living if you're a touring professional. Her misses weren't as bad as the average player's, because she has a good of pair of hands and she'd worked hard with those hands to control the club face through impact. However, her competition wasn't average players. The weeks when she didn't make many mistakes, got some good bounces, and her hand-eye coordination was particularly sharp, she'd make the cut and a check. Otherwise, it was "down the road," as they say on tour.

When I started working with her, she had several problems. First, she was aiming to the right. Second, she was taking the club back inside and rotating her forearms. At the top, her left wrist was flat and the club was laid off behind her. Then she was bringing the club down farther inside (what I call an inside loop) and re-rotating her forearms to square the club face at impact; otherwise she would have hit everything to the right.

Now, that's a complicated golf swing. When her timing was good, and with those good hands, she could play. But when it wasn't . . . well, you can imagine. When she missed it right, the result was a weak block. When she missed it left, the result was a hook, and those were the ones that scared her. As Lee Trevino said, "You can talk to a fade, but those hooks won't listen."

The first time I worked with Maggie, she'd just suffered through a period of hooking the ball and was really fanning the club open going back, attempting to keep it in play. But that's like trying to make a right from two wrongs.

I started the rebuilding project by squaring her stance. Of course, Maggie thought everything would go left at first, but her "optics" soon adjusted.

Next, I taught her how to get to the top correctly. I took her up vertically, making sure her wrists cocked naturally into a cupped position. I even carried the shaft across the line more than she would ever be able to because she'd been so laid off before. (Bobby Jones called that the "principle of correction by exaggeration," something I think every pro should have in his toolbox.)

Then I told her to bring the club down vertically, instead of from behind her back. It took a few swings, but when she caught one solid, she told me the sensations were of using less hands and hitting the ball more with her turn. Just what I wanted to hear.

That was the beginning of teaching a slight, ninety-eight-pound lady to use the big muscles of her legs and hips to hit the ball rather than the small muscles of her hands and arms. And you should see her smoke 'em now.

However, I don't want to leave you with the impression that it was easy. Maggie had to work very hard, because at first it was comfortable for her to slip back into her old way of swinging, of rotating her forearms and laying the club off with the left wrist flat and the right palm facing up. But today she turns beautifully and swings the club up vertically. At the top, her hands are under the shaft, her left wrist is cupped naturally, and the knuckles of her right hand point skyward. From there it's a simple matter for her to bring the club down on-line with her lower body and deliver it squarely into the back of the ball.

Maggie has always been a fierce competitor, in spite of her sweet, girl-next-door demeanor. Now she hits it long and straight, no longer putting so much pressure on her excellent short game. As far as I'm concerned, she's the best little player in the world.

There are two principal methods to hit a golf ball, in my opinion—the forearm-rotation swing and the body-rotation or centrifugal-force swing that I teach (it's been called the drag-back swing, too). Each has produced fine play through the years and each has won championships. The big problem with the forearm-rotation swing, as I see it, is that it's more complicated.

Recently, an older journeyman professional, whom I'll call Bob, came to me on the sly for help. That's not his real name, but his regular instructor, who's also a close friend of his, teaches the forearm-rotation swing, and Bob didn't want him to know he'd been to see someone else.

For months, Bob had been visiting the left rough of too many holes, and his scores were reflecting it. He'd been missing cuts, and whatever advice his friend gave him only seemed to work for a round or two.

Golf is such a game of opposites. Because Bob had been hooking the ball, he felt that by weakening his grip, he would be able to bring the club down slightly open and thus reduce the number of shots that went left. When I first saw him, his left hand was on the side of the shaft and his right hand was on top of it at address. But all he was really doing with that grip was compounding the problem with extra hand and arm rotation to keep the ball from flying weakly to the right.

The solution was to get his hands on the club naturally, and of course the first thing he said was something like "Good God! I'll rope-hook it into the next time zone with this grip."

"Not if you don't rotate your hands and arms," I said calmly, having heard that type of comment before. "If you keep your hands passive and swing the club with your lower body, the face will come down squarely."

From his expression, I could tell he didn't believe me. So I showed him how to take it back in one piece with his hips, rather than with the quick forearm rollover he'd been using. Then I carried him to the top by standing the club up and cocking his wrists into the cupped position.

"Now bring it down by rotating your hips, not your fore-arms."

Somehow he mustered up the courage to try it, and on the first swing he hit it square and long with good trajectory.

"Heavens! You don't think it was beginner's luck, do you?"

"I doubt it, but the only way to be sure is to hit some more."

Well, Bob kept hitting balls, and soon a pattern developed. When his upper body remained passive, the result was flush contact with the ball starting on a line either at the target or just right of it and drawing slightly at the end. However, when he slipped back to his old swing and tried to add something extra with his hands, the result was always a hook.

The ideal shot, in my opinion, is one with a little draw, and I gauge a person's ability to score by the amount of curve his ball has on it. The good players usually don't bend the ball much. However, golfers who rotate their hands and arms seem to curve it more in both directions than golfers who don't. So, as I see it, the less you use your hands and arms through impact, the more accurate your shots will be.

With the swing I teach, you might say that the club face remains "in the address position" at all times, because there's no movement of the upper body independent of the lower body's turn. When you roll your forearms, however, the club face moves independently of the lower body and is no longer in the address position.

Another indication of the difference in Bob's ball-striking was the shape of his divots. Whenever he rotated just his hips and not his forearms, they were shaped like a dollar bill, like this:

It's a rectangle with square corners, because the club face remains square to the target line through impact. You produce this type of divot when your hands are passive. The leading edge of the club head goes into the turf square and comes out square. Whenever Bob cut a divot that looked like that, he hit a good shot.

But when he used his hands actively, he cut toed-in divots, as I call them. They're shaped like this:

A toed-in divot means you've rolled the club head through impact by rotating your forearms. It also means that you're making the swing more complicated than it needs to be.

By the time we'd finished the lesson, Bob was cutting dollar-bill-shaped divots with almost every swing. It must have been an omen, because he finished on the leader board at every tournament for the next six weeks.

He called me one night and said, "John, I swear I haven't hit the ball like this since I was a kid!"

"Sounds like you're having a good time."

"I'm having a great time! But I have to be honest with you. With this swing, I'm a little concerned sometimes that one's going to get away from me."

Amazing. My swing had put more money in his bank account in a month and a half than his old swing had in the last year, and he was worried.

"Well, Bob, the way I look at it, one's going to get away from you every now and then no matter what type of swing you use."

"True."

"And hasn't your percentage of good shots increased since you stopped rotating your hands and arms?"

"No question about it."

"Then if I were you, I wouldn't change a thing."

He didn't, and he's having a good year, his best in a long time.

Paul begins the swing with a level, stationary hip turn, as if he were turning in a barrel. His passive upper body reacts by moving back in one piece.

As his hands approach waist height, he stands the club up with his left wrist cocking into a cupped position. Note that his left shoulder is turning *up* to his chin.

At the top, Paul has made a full hip turn because his left rear pants pocket is facing the target. His right knee has remained flexed and it's still positioned inside his right ankle. A full hip turn allows a full shoulder turn, and note how level his shoulders have turned.

A re-turn of the hips while the club is still swinging up starts the downswing. Because Paul's hands are passive and aren't putting pressure on the side of the shaft, his wrists remain cocked until centrifugal force and the conservation of angular momentum release the club head, slamming it into the back of the ball.

With the ball on its way, the momentum of Paul's turning body and swinging arms pull him onto his left side.

He finishes balanced on his left foot with his hips and shoulders level.

How to Practice and How to Prepare to Hit a Shot on the Course

To buy this book, you had to spend some money. Now, reading it, you're spending your time. In other words, you're making an investment in your game, and if you're like the typical investor, you expect a reasonable return. To help you realize that return, in terms of a better swing and lower scores on the course, I've included the material in this chapter.

How to Practice

To become an accomplished player, you must practice. There is no alternative. However, the way you practice is as important as how much you practice. I recommend not only that you practice a lot but that you practice with purpose.

Practicing with purpose means you should put as much thought and effort into every ball you hit on the practice tee as you do into balls you hit on the course. Mindlessly beating range balls, in my opinion, usually does more harm than good. I believe that you play the way you practice. If you practice sloppy, chances are you'll play sloppy. But concentrate on every swing and you'll quickly see improvement.

Should you find yourself with an hour or more to work on your game, arrange the session so that you stay alert and focused. For example, don't just stand there and machine-gun a pile of balls. Work on your full swing until you feel tired or sense you're losing your edge, then go chip or putt for a while. When your attention starts to wander on the practice putting green, come back and work on your full swing again. That way you'll get the most benefit from your time.

You should constantly review the preliminary fundamentals of grip, alignment, posture, weight distribution, and ball position as you practice. This is where a pre-shot routine comes in, which I'll describe in some detail in a minute. Think of it as a checklist to take care of the preliminaries. And by using a pre-shot routine with every swing on the range, you'll quickly make it a part of your game on the course. I would also suggest that you never hit a practice shot without laying a club down parallel to the target line to make sure of your alignment.

It's a good idea to work on only one of the dynamic fundamentals at once. For instance, concentrate just on making a slow, deliberate takeaway. Or focus on your hips, turning them so the left rear pants pocket faces the target, then the right front one faces the target. Or think about swinging the club up to the top with a turn of your hips, then leaving it there as you re-turn your hips.

When you do hit a good practice shot, don't immediately reach for another ball. Take a moment to let the sensations you felt while making that swing sink in; try to ingest them mentally. You can retain sensory information just as you can memorize a telephone number, a recipe, or directions to a golf course you haven't played before.

So, practice a lot and practice with purpose. Before each swing, think about what you're trying to accomplish, then use a pre-shot routine to take care of the preliminaries and stay focused. If you hit a particularly good one, take a moment and let the way it felt sink in.

You'll be hitting it with your practice swing in no time!

The Pre-shot Routine

An important key to good play is repetition, especially where it concerns your preparation to hit shots. Setting up the same way every time is the best way to make sure that you're setting up correctly, and if you're confident that your setup is correct, you can give full attention to the sensations of the swing.

Watch the top-level players. They go through the same routine for every shot. Taking care of the preliminaries is a habit with them, something they do almost subconsciously, so they can mentally focus on the shot itself. Here's the pre-shot routine I use, and I recommend that you use it or one like it.

First, I start by standing about six feet directly behind the ball, club in hand, looking down the intended line of the shot. From this position, I decide what type of shot best suits the situation, then I take a moment to visualize it.

Next, I pick out two spots, one about a foot or so behind the ball and the other a foot or so in front of it. Both are located on the target line. They can be anything—a discolored blade of grass, a broken tee, even an old divot—just as long as they were already there and you don't move them. (The rules of golf won't allow you to create a mark to indicate the line of play.)

Next, I take three normal steps, moving around the ball to the left, keeping my eyes on the line, not the target. I always take three steps and begin with my left foot. It might be more than that for you, depending on the length of your stride and how far behind the ball you started from. Regardless, make sure your steps are normal ones, because they provide you with a measure for the maximum width of your stance. Of course, if you're hitting a club other than your driver, you'll need to move your feet closer together, especially for the short irons.

Using the two spots I picked out, I mentally connect them with a line through the ball and align my feet, knees, hips, and shoulders parallel to that line. Then I carefully place the leading edge of the club head squarely behind the ball. Accurate alignment is very important, and I take my time doing it.

At this point, I double-check my ball position. Remember, 7-iron shots are played in the middle of the stance. With longer clubs the ball is moved forward in half-inch increments, and with shorter clubs backward in half-inch increments.

I also check the distance I'm standing from the ball. With my arms hanging relaxed, the club head should rest directly behind the ball. Usually that means that the butt of the club will be no more than a handspan from my thigh.

If all is in order, I swivel my head so my eyes can look down the target line. Then I begin my waggle, visualizing the shot again and sensing the swing I need to make to produce it. After that, I kick-start the swing with a forward press, knowing I've done all I can do to make the shot a success, and freewheel it from there.

If something isn't right—perhaps I've been distracted or the wind has started blowing and I'm no longer sure of my club selection—I'll back away and regroup. Once I've resolved the problem, I'll step behind the ball again and start my pre-shot routine over from the beginning.

If you haven't been using a pre-shot routine, this may seem complicated at first, but it's not. After you've built it into your game and made a habit of it, you'll be taking care of the preparations automatically, leaving your mind uncluttered so that you can focus on the execution of the shot itself on a more sensory level. And the best way to make it a habit is to use a pre-shot routine every time you swing the club, whether it's on the course or on the driving range.

PUTTING

In a few paragraphs, I'm going to turn this chapter over to one of the best putters on the PGA Tour, Paul Azinger, and let him tell you how he putts. First, however, I want to share my thoughts with you on this most illusive part of the game. Paul developed his technique to cope with the slick, fast greens that the tour players face each week. But not every course has those, and besides, there's more than one way of approaching this activity some have called a game within the game.

For me, putting is a miniature of the full swing. It's a pendulum stroke, just like the one you make with your driver or 5-iron or pitching wedge. The major difference is that the lower body isn't needed to supply power for a putt, because you're only moving the ball a relatively short distance. (Actually, on long lag putts, it's a good idea to use your lower body some. Otherwise, you really have to whack it with your hands and arms, and it's difficult to keep the putt on line when you do that.)

Here's some of the things I've noticed that most good putters do.

A good putter always finds a comfortable, balanced way to stand so that he can see the line. For some, that means leaning over; for others, standing up straight. He usually holds the putter gently with passive hands. He takes it back low, never picking it up, although on longer putts it will come off the ground some.

Keeping his head very still throughout the stroke, he swings the putter back slightly inside the line, then swings it forward on the same path, with the face of the putter always square. His backswing and follow-through are usually about the same length, and his tempo is always pendulum-like. Several good putters have also told me that they keep their left shoulder low through the stroke, which helps them stay down and keeps the putter on-line longer.

In the realm of general advice, I would offer this. First, don't be afraid to experiment with different grips and stances. Find what's comfortable and what works for you. Second, practice. Practice your putting as much as you practice anything else.

If I had to choose one adjective that applies to all the good putters I've even known, it would be "confident." Confidence is the product of a two-step process. First, you learn good mechanics. Second, you practice those mechanics until you develop an acute sense of touch on the greens. When that happens, you'll think you can sink everything. You won't, of course, but you'll make a lot more of them than the next guy.

Now, here's someone who does make a lot more of them than the next guy.

How I Putt

by Paul Azinger

Putting is nearly half the game of golf.

For that reason alone, it's crucial, even if it does involve the shortest stroke.

On the Tour, putting is what separates the contenders from the pretenders. By that I don't mean to imply there are bad putters out here, because there aren't. Some are just better than others, and the players whose names appear on the leader board week after week are exceptionally good.

Not only do you strike far more putts in a round than any other type of shot, but with a "hot" putter you can take advantage of scoring opportunities like holing a birdie after a good approach or saving par with a one-putt when you've played poorly from tee to green. The higher your aspirations, the more proficient you'll have to be with the putter.

For instance, how many putts per round do you think a player needs to average if he wants to be a scratch golfer? Thirty-six? Thirty-three? Thirty? Twenty-seven? Even if you're a good ball-striker, you'll need to average about thirty per round, or, in other words, six one-putts and no three-putts. That's because even the better players usually hit only about twelve of eighteen greens in regulation. If your aspirations aren't quite that high, but you still want to post lower numbers (and who doesn't?), improving your putting is the quickest way to do it.

I qualified for the tour primarily on the strength of the tee-to-green game John Redman taught me. My putting was inconsistent because, like many of my amateur partners in the Wednesday pro-ams, I took the putter back a long way and decelerated at the ball. I've since changed my grip, shortened my backswing, and trained myself to accelerate the putter through

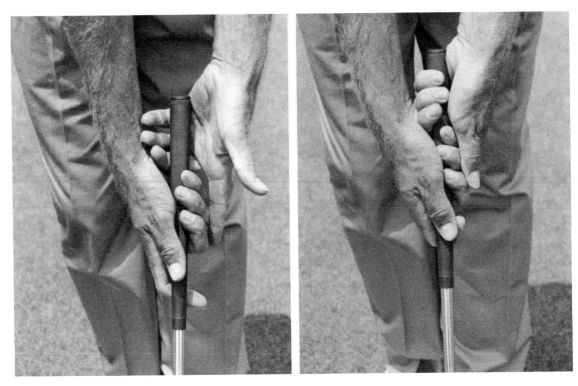

Paul Azinger's grip. Unusual-looking, but effective.

the ball. As a result, I've climbed from near the bottom of the Tour's putting statistics to near the top. If you're not satisfied with your putting, I would recommend my method without hesitation.

This is how I did it.

First, I altered the way I held the putter. My old grip was a regular overlap grip, similar to the way most people hold their woods and irons. However, with a putter, my hands seemed too far apart and didn't work well together. Also, I had a problem with my left wrist breaking down. So I changed to a reverse overlap grip, which brought my hands closer together. I turned my hands more underneath so that the palms faced outward. This helped lock the wrists in place, and I took my left thumb off the shaft and laid it over the fingers of the right hand.

It may look unusual, but it's effective. The result is a stroke in which my arms, wrists, hands, and putter work together as a single unit.

Next, I shortened my backstroke, using several drills. The first involved pushing the ball. I would simply set the putter down behind the ball and push it into the cup. From two feet away, I had to make twenty in a row. If I missed, I started over.

With the second drill, I took the putter back as short as I could and tried to hit the ball as many times as I could before the ball went into the hole. Again I worked from two feet away and had to make twenty in a row or start over. You can imagine

Paul's first putting drill—pushing the ball.

**Paul's second drill—hitting the ball
as many times as he can.**

how hard I concentrated on those last five or six. As a consequence, my backstroke became very short and I trained myself to
accelerate on the follow-through.

For the third drill, I would have to make twenty in a row
from two feet with my regular stroke, knowing that a miss
meant (you guessed it) starting over. After I'd completed those, I
would move back to six feet and stay there until I made ten in a
row.

The purpose of all this was to develop a simple and effective
putting stroke that was repeatable under pressure. The best way
to accomplish that, I thought, was by the repetition of good mechanics while feeling some self-imposed psychological stress.

Paul's putting stroke is a pendulum-type motion with the arms, hands, and putter swinging as a unit.

Paul's putting stance is
comfortable and he's aligned
slightly open with his eyes
directly over the ball.

There were days when I was able to finish these drills in no time and other days when it took me hours. Obviously, you have to be dedicated to do it, but I'll guarantee that it will make you a better putter.

Today, my stroke is an accelerating one, with a short, compact backswing and a longer follow-through straight toward the hole. It's still a stroke, too, not a jab, with a pendulum-type tempo. All phases of my putting have improved because of it, and I have many rounds now in which I haven't missed any putts I thought I should have made. My shorter putts stay on line better, because they're struck with more authority and because I'm following through toward the hole with an accelerating stroke. When you decelerate, the putter tends to waver as it approaches the ball. More medium-length putts are going in because I'm striking them precisely. With a shorter backstroke, I'm not as likely to get the putter off-line and miss the sweet spot. And because I'm striking putts more precisely, I'm a better judge of distance, the result being that my lag putting has improved. Contrary to what you may have thought, you don't need to take the putter back a long way to be a good lag putter.

From the thirty-to-forty-foot range, obviously you're not going to make a lot of putts, so your objective should be to two-putt as many times as possible. To do that, you've got to develop a good sense of speed, and it's easier to do that with a short, compact backstroke, because there are fewer variables.

Concerning the other fundamentals, I don't have a lot to say about them, not because they're unimportant, but because there's just not much to say.

Your stance should be a comfortable one. Good putting is primarily feel. If your stance is comfortable, you're more apt to be relaxed, and if you're relaxed, you'll be better able to sense the stroke you need to make. Also, your stance should allow you to swing your shoulders, arms, hands, and putter as a unit.

As for alignment, most good putters stand with their bodies either parallel to the intended line or slightly open to it, with their eyes directly over the ball.

Summary

A good putting stroke should be a pendulum-type motion with a cadence. I recommend one with a short, compact backswing and a longer, accelerating follow-through toward the hole. Use a grip in which your hands are close together so that your shoulders, arms, hands, and putter can work together as a unit.

Stances vary. Make sure yours is a comfortable one, so you'll be relaxed when you putt. Align your body either parallel to the line or slightly open to it with your eyes over the ball.

Develop a dependable putting stroke by repeating good fundamentals while feeling some self-imposed pressure, like having to make a certain number of practice putts in a row. To do that, use my practice drills or develop some of your own.

CHIPPING

When it comes to shaving strokes off your score, the ability to chip the ball accurately is almost as valuable as being good with your putter. I define a chip shot as one from just off the putting surface where there's only short grass between you and the green and your lie is a good one.

As I'm sure you realize by now, I'm something of a fanatic when it comes to keeping things simple, and my method of chipping couldn't be less complicated. I recommend using the same club for most chip shots and approaching each as an enlarged putt, not an abridged full swing. You get solid results more quickly this way.

By using one club, you can develop more confidence and raise your comfort level. I prefer a pitching wedge, but a 9-iron or 8-iron might also be a good choice. It depends on the individual. If you have confidence with a club, you're more relaxed with it in your hands, and that counts for a lot around the green, when your touch must be exact. Using one club also eliminates doubts that can ruin your concentration.

At address, you want your feet rather close together, and your stance should be slightly open. I use my regular grip, but some people use their putting grip when chipping and get good results. I'd recommend that you use whatever works best for you. You should choke down an inch or two (the shorter the shot, the more you choke down) and hold the club lightly. Allow your arms to hang relaxed.

To find the correct ball position, take a few practice strokes and clip some grass. Where the club makes contact with the turf in relation to your feet is the low point of the downswing arc, and you want to play the ball just behind the low point. Normally that will be inside your back foot. You also want your hands slightly ahead of the ball at address, and of course you

For a chip shot, the ball is positioned off the right foot with the hands ahead of the club head.

The wrists cock slightly, if at all.

want the leading edge of the club aligned square to the target. It's important that you keep about 60 percent of your weight on your front foot. The combination of your hands slightly ahead of the club and your weight favoring your left foot ensures a descending blow and solid contact.

The swing itself is similar to a putt, with the shoulders, arms, hands, and club moving as a single unit, like a pendulum. The difference is that with a chip shot, just as with a full swing, the hips generate the motion. Think of it as a putting stroke with legs.

You swing the club back by turning your lower body slightly,

The right wrist angle is still evident. No scoop!

The club-face alignment is the same as at address.

The chipping stance is slightly open, with the arms close to the body.

The club face is square to the back of the ball.

then swing it through by re-turning your lower body. It's not a big movement, but it's enough to swing your arms. The backswing and downswing should be approximately the same length. The wrists shouldn't hinge much, if at all, and at impact your hands should be slightly ahead of the club, as if you were gently brushing the ball toward the target. I would strongly recommend that you try to see the club and ball make contact.

By using your lower body to generate motion, you can keep your hands relaxed and passive so that your sense of touch is

The lower body has delivered the club to the ball with knee and hip action.

With the ball on its way, there is no sign of hand or forearm rotation.

keen. Also, the club face remains square to the target longer, meaning consistently better results. Players who use their hands actively to hit chip shots tend to rotate the club, and that cuts down on the time it's aligned square. When their hand-eye coordination is off, they have trouble chipping the ball on-line.

Treat a chip like a putt in terms of judging how hard to strike the ball. You do want to land the ball on the green, but don't be concerned with how far to hit it in the air versus how far it should roll. Keep it simple. Think about making a pendulum stroke, with the length of your backswing and downswing determining the overall length of the shot. That's the quickest way to develop a sense of the force needed for a particular shot.

I recommend one-club chipping because you get good results faster with it than with any other method. For most people, that's important, because they don't have a lot of time to practice. If you always use the same club, it's always the same feel, and with the same feel, it's easy to improvise. There have been some exceptional players who chipped with just one club.

If you do have the luxury of a lot of practice time, there's a multi-club technique that a lot of professionals use and that you may want to try. The rationale behind it is that it's easier to roll the ball than to pitch it. This is how it works.

Select the club that has the least amount of loft that will allow you to fly the ball just onto the green and then roll it to the cup. For example, suppose you're five feet off the putting surface and the pin is twenty feet away. You select an 8-iron, because through trial and error you know that if you carry the ball one-fourth of the way, it will roll the remaining three-fourths. In other words, your carry-to-roll ratio is one to three with that particular club. If the shot involves a ten-foot carry and a ten-foot roll, you would use your pitching wedge, because by practicing with it you know that the carry-to-roll ratio with your wedge is one to one. With your 6-iron, it might be one to six, and so on.

The multi-club approach can be effective *if* (and that's a big if) you have a lot of time to practice. Its proponents argue that it's simple because you make the same swing but with different clubs. I think it's complicated, because each club has a different feel and each is a different length. Choking down on the longer ones doesn't help, because that changes their effective swing weight. If you use more than one club to chip with, you'll have to get comfortable with each of them to be good.

With the one-club method, it's the same club, the same feel, and when you practice, all you're doing is learning to hit the ball different distances. It takes an extreme situation for me to chip with something other than my pitching wedge, like when I'm two feet off the green and the cup's sixty feet away. If I can't use my putter, I might use a more steep-faced club, say a 6-iron. Or when I have very little green to work with, I might chip it with a sand wedge. But nine times out of ten, I'll pull the same club from the bag.

Summary

For saving strokes around the green, chipping is an essential skill to develop. I'd recommend that you treat each chip shot as an enlarged putting stroke rather than an abridged full swing.

Your stance should be a narrow one, with your feet slightly open to the target. I use my regular grip when chipping, but some people get better results with their putting grip. Use what works best for you, but regardless of the grip you use, hold the club lightly and choke down. Position the ball just inside your back foot and place more of your weight, say 60 percent, on your front foot. Your hands should be slightly ahead of the club face at address.

As with the full swing, the hips generate all motion. Swing the club back by turning your hips to the right, then swing it through by re-turning your hips to the left. The shoulders, arms, hands, and club move as a single unit. There's little if any wrist break with a chip shot. At impact, just as at address, your hands should be slightly ahead of the club face for crisp contact.

The quickest and simplest way to become a good chipper is to use one club. With one club, it's always the same feel, so all your practice time is spent learning one thing—how hard to hit the ball for shots of different distances.

PITCHING

I define a pitch shot as anything less than a full swing with a lofted club when you're trying to fly the ball to a certain spot, usually on the green. The ball will roll once it lands, but you're primarily concerned with its carry. From around the putting surface, you might elect to pitch the ball when a chip shot isn't appropriate. For instance, there might be trouble between you and the green, like a sand trap or a grass bunker. Or maybe there's a mound or severe depression on the green itself and the easier shot is to loft the ball over it. From farther back, say twenty, fifty, even a hundred yards away, the pitch shot (as opposed to the pitch-and-run, which I'll discuss shortly) is used most of the time on modern courses with their softer greens.

In the section on chipping, I recommended that you approach the chip shot not as an abridged full swing, but as an enlarged putt with your lower body generating the motion. The pitch shot, however, I consider to be an abridged full swing. All of the full-swing fundamentals are there.

You hold the club lightly with your natural grip. Your stance should be narrow, with your alignment square to the target or slightly open, and most of your weight should be on your left side. Allow your arms to hang relaxed. This is another active-lower-body/passive-upper-body shot.

The ball is positioned back in your stance, but not as far back as with the chip shot, because height is important. The best way to find the exact spot to place it is by taking a practice swing and clipping the turf. That's the low point of your arc, and that's where you should position the ball in relation to your feet. You want to strike the ball first, but just barely.

The takeaway is initiated with a hip turn, just as in the full swing. Remember Horace Hutchinson's advice—slow back! The hips turn your shoulders, the shoulders swing your arms, and the club swings back and up. As your hands approach waist height, your wrists should cock. This is the major difference between the chip shot and the pitch shot. With a chip, there's little if any wrist cock. However, cocking your wrists on a pitch shot enables you to strike the ball a more descending blow, which gives it a higher trajectory.

The downswing is initiated by re-turning your hips, which swings the arms down and pulls the club through with them. As with a full swing, you allow centrifugal force to uncock your wrists in the hitting area. Do not try to use the club like a lever by putting pressure on the side of the shaft to make the club head move. That's the duffer's way of doing it. To help ensure that your hands remain passive, think about them being slightly ahead of the club face at impact.

With the ball on its way, the momentum of your swinging arms will pull you gently around your left side. As in the full swing, there is a redistribution of your weight, but it's the result of the swing and not something you try to make happen.

The key to hitting good pitch shots of varying length is *learning to control the distance of the shot with your lower body*. It takes practice, but it's the most accurate and repeatable way to do it, especially under pressure.

When learning the shot, I would slip out of the pro shop during slack times and go to the practice range, where I had set up targets at fifteen, thirty, forty-five, and seventy-five yards. Taking half a backswing, I would hit shots to those targets using hip speed to gauge the distance, just like throwing a ball. It was some of the best practice time I've ever spent, and I strongly encourage you to do the same. Not only will it help ingrain the fundamentals, but it will make you a deadly accurate wedge player, especially under pressure.

There are two special pitch shots that need to be mentioned—the lob and the pitch-and-run.

The lob is a high-trajectory, quick-stopping type of shot. It's a great one to have in your repertoire when there's a sand trap between you and the pin and you don't have much green to work with.

To hit the lob, you need a reasonable lie, because you must slide the leading edge of the club under the ball. Use a sand wedge and weaken your grip by rotating your hands to the left on the club about 15 to 20 degrees. That will open the face and increase its effective loft. Open your stance and position the ball at the bottom of your downswing arc. Again, you determine that point by taking a practice swing or two, clipping the turf, then walking into that ball position. Your weight should be evenly distributed.

Using your lower body to generate all motion, swing along the line of your stance so that the club comes down steeply from outside the target line. To ensure that the club remains open, hold the club lightly and keep the back of your left hand facing skyward as you follow through.

The lob takes practice, but it can bail you out of jail when nothing else will work.

The pitch-and-run is a commonly used approach shot in Scotland, where the courses are usually firm and the greens unprotected in front. As a consequence, the Scots are exceptionally skillful at pitching the ball short of the putting surface and rolling it onto the green. In America, it's a good shot to use when the flag is on the top tier of a two-tiered green and flying the ball all the way back is risky.

It's a simple shot to hit if you practice it and get some idea of

For the pitch shot, position the ball at the low point of your downswing arc.

Start the takeaway with a hip turn and stand the club up as you swing it back.

how far the ball will roll after it lands. I'd recommend that you use a club with less loft than your pitching wedge, say your 8- or 9-iron, and play the ball back in your stance.

Summary

Think of the pitch shot as an abridged full swing.

As in the full swing, you hold the club lightly with your natural grip. Use a narrow stance and align yourself either parallel to the target line or slightly open to it, with your weight favoring your left side. Allow your arms to hang relaxed, with your hands ahead of the club face. The ball is positioned back in your stance, at the low point of your downswing arc.

Start the takeaway with your hips. Your passive shoulders will respond by turning, causing your arms to swing the club

The downswing is triggered by a re-turn of the hips which pulls the arms down and the club along with them.

Let centrifugal force and the club head's momentum uncock your wrists in the hitting area.

Finish the swing balanced on your left foot.

back and up. As the hands approach waist height, your wrists will cock.

The downswing is also initiated by your hips. They re-turn toward the target, pulling your arms and the club down. At impact, your hands should feel slightly ahead of the club face.

The key to hitting pitch shots of varying length is learning to control the distance of the shot with the speed of your hips, and that takes practice.

The lob and the pitch-and-run are two special types of pitch shot.

The lob is a high-trajectory pitch that lands softly and doesn't roll much. To hit it, you need a good lie. Open your stance and weaken your grip so that the club's loft is increased. I'd recommend that you use a sand wedge. Distribute your weight evenly. Swing the club along the line of your stance and across the target line from the outside. To ensure that the club face remains open through the shot, hold the club lightly and on the follow-through keep the back of your left hand facing skyward.

To hit a pitch-and-run, use a club with less loft than your pitching wedge, like an 8- or 9-iron, and play the ball back in your stance.

SAND SHOTS

Contrary to what a lot of amateurs think, the routine sand shot from a good, level lie in a greenside bunker is an easy shot to play. With a few adjustments because of the sand, it's basically your normal pitch-shot swing in which you're hitting the sand behind the ball instead of the ball itself. And if you can remember two things, it's a piece of cake. Just swing deliberately and make sure you finish the swing.

Here are the adjustments you need to make.

First, open your stance by aligning your feet and shoulders left of the target as much as 25–30 degrees, and position the ball forward, just inside the left heel. Work your feet down into the sand to feel its depth and texture and so you'll be swinging from a firm foundation.

Next, weaken your grip slightly, turning your hands to the left a couple of degrees, and choke down toward the steel, because your body is now lower in relation to the ball. Your posture should be the same as with a routine pitch shot. Your knees should be flexed and remain flexed throughout the swing, and your arms should hang relaxed as you bend forward from the waist. Also, your weight should favor your left side.

This, like the pitch shot, is an active-lower-body/passive-upper-body shot. Start the swing by turning your hips. The shoulders, arms, and hands will follow. At waist height, your wrists should hinge as you stand the club up. Make sure your tempo is deliberate. This is no time to be in a hurry. (As a matter of fact, I've found sand shots easier to play the slower I swing.) Then turn back to the ball, with the hips leading. By the way, don't look at the ball—keep your eye on a spot in the sand a couple of inches behind it where you want to hit.

Because your shoulders are aligned open, your arms will au-

For sand shots, the stance is wider for stability, and the feet are firmly planted.

There's only a small turn of the hips. Note the club's vertical position.

tomatically swing with your body, on a line left of the target. This swing path, combined with an open club face, brings the club down in a U shape and allows your sand wedge to make a shallow cut under the ball. The ball should pop out, riding on a handful of sand as it flies toward the target. Be sure to finish the swing; don't just hit the sand and stop. Also, think about keeping your hands ahead of the club face through impact. That will prevent scooping or hitting the ball with the right hand, producing a deep gouge rather than a shallow cut.

To get a feeling for the sand shot, step into a practice bunker

The hips have cleared and the club is facing skyward.

The finish is balanced and the hips and shoulders are still level.

and take some practice swings *without* a ball in front of you. Just take full, deliberate swings, letting the wide flange of the sand wedge bounce the club through the sand. To keep from decelerating, think about making your backswing and downswing the same length.

Once you've become comfortable doing that, drop a few balls at your feet and splash them out, as if each is just a big grain of sand. *At first, don't pay any attention to where they're going. Your objective is to get them out, nothing more.* Remember—swing slow and finish your swing. Only after you've developed some confidence should you start thinking about distance and direc-

The body is aligned to the left of the target line to produce an outside-in plane.

The head is steady and the body is braced.

tion. Direction, of course, is a function of your alignment. Distance you control with the length of your backswing and hip speed, just as for the pitch shot.

If the only type of lie we ever got in a bunker was a good level one, they wouldn't be considered hazards. That isn't the case, however, as I'm sure you know. There are also buried lies and uphill, downhill, and sidehill lies, and the texture of the sand changes, especially when it's wet. Not all bunkers are near the green, either; sometimes you've got to play long bunker shots, perhaps the game's toughest shot.

For a buried lie, square up both your stance and the club

The lower body has cleared, and the club has sliced the ball out.

The hands and arms have followed the hips without turning over.

When the ball is buried, it is positioned farther back and the stance is narrower, more like the stance for a full wedge shot.

The wrists cock more at the top.

face. A shallow divot won't work this time. You'll still need to choke down on the grip to compensate for having worked your feet into the sand. Hold the club more firmly and swing it up abruptly, then bring it down steeply, striking the sand just behind the ball. You have to chop the ball out of this type of lie. Allow for extra roll, because the ball will come out with no backspin.

The key to playing from an uphill lie in a bunker is to swing

The club is swung down steeply by a strong hip and leg drive.

For this buried lie, Paul leaves the club head in the sand.

the club along the contour of the sand. To do that, you align your shoulders parallel to the surface by putting most of your weight on your back foot. That lets you lean back. Then you simply swing the club up the slope, striking the sand several inches behind the ball. Most golfers instinctively want to lean into the slope, and they usually bury the club head in the face of the slope and leave the ball in the sand.

For a downhill lie, you also swing the club along the contour of the sand. Place most of your weight on your front foot and lean forward so that your shoulders are parallel to the slope. You'll need to position the ball back in your stance and make a rather steep downswing to ensure that you hit the sand behind the ball and not the ball itself. The downhill lie is a tougher shot than the uphill lie.

When the ball is below your feet, increase your knee flex. The danger is raising up on the downswing and blading the ball, so make sure you maintain that flex throughout the swing. You'll need to aim farther left of the hole, because the ball will fly out to the right.

When the ball is above your feet, stand up straight and choke down on the club. Aim farther right, because the ball will come out to the left.

For wet, hard-packed, or coarse-grained sand, use your pitching wedge. The pitching wedge has a smaller flange, so its leading edge will cut into the sand and take a divot, not bounce into the ball. If the sand is very fine or powdery, open the face of your sand wedge 45 degrees or more and concentrate on making a shallow cut. With powdery sand, it's easy to cut too deeply and leave the ball in the bunker.

The consensus among golf's best players is that of all the shots in the game, the long bunker shot is the toughest, because its margin of allowable error is so small. With a routine sand shot from close around the green, you can miss the spot behind the ball you were trying to hit by an inch or more and still get a good result. That's not the case, however, with a bunker shot of thirty yards or more. You must make a bigger swing because of the distance involved and strike the sand precisely.

This is how to play it.

Align yourself slightly open to the target, square up the club face, and position the ball back in your stance. Your weight should favor your left side. Then use your normal pitch-shot swing, striking the sand about an inch behind the ball. Again, make sure you finish. If you have a good lie on firm sand, you can even hit the ball first, playing it just like a pitch shot. Either way, this shot requires a lot of practice to develop a feel for distance. For the really long bunker shots, say fifty yards or more, use your 8- or 9-iron instead of your sand wedge.

From a fairway trap, where a full swing is involved, you can play either a high cut shot or a low punch shot if your lie is a good one and the lip on the bunker isn't a problem.

To hit a cut shot, open your stance slightly by aligning both your feet and shoulders left of the target. Position the ball forward an inch. Remember to work your feet into the sand so you won't slip and to choke down on the club. Also, select a club one longer than what you would normally use for a shot of that length, because you'll lose about half a club's length of distance. Besides, you'll get better results if you don't try to go at it hard but make an easy, balanced swing. On the takeaway, alter your normal swing path by routing the club back and up on a plane outside the target line. On the downswing, bring the club down steeply from outside that line, making sure to strike the ball first and not the sand.

To play a punch shot, you want your shoulders aligned square to the target, but your feet and hips should be open about 20 degrees. Position the ball back in your stance about two inches. As with the cut shot, select one club longer than you would normally use from that particular distance, but this time it's because you're only going to make a three-quarter swing. Again, work your feet into the sand for firm footing and choke down. At address, your hands should be ahead of the club face, and they should remain that way at impact. The punch shot, like everything else I teach, is a lower-body shot. The hands and arms remain relaxed and passive throughout. On the backswing, make only half of a hip turn, which will allow your shoulders to turn about three-quarters. Your hands shouldn't swing higher than your shoulders. On the downswing, re-turn your hips toward the target, with the upper body following. You should strike the ball first, not the sand, the same as with the cut shot. However, the ball's trajectory will be much lower. You should finish with all of your weight on your left side and your belt buckle facing the target. However, the follow-through with your arms should be only about three-quarters of a full follow-through. The punch shot from a good lie in a fairway bunker is a good one to use when you have some green to work with. It's also good to use from anywhere when it's windy.

If your ball is buried, however, or the front lip of the fairway trap is high enough to prevent you from going at the green, then your sole objective should be to get the ball out and back to the fairway. Don't compound your mistake by trying some risky shot with a small chance of success. You can still make a par with a one-putt, and you certainly don't want to turn a bogey into something worse. Tommy Armour used to say that you should play the shot you've got the best chance of playing well, and you should play this shot so that the next one will be easy. That's good advice anytime, but particularly under these circumstances.

Summary

The routine sand shot from a green-side bunker is actually the pitch-shot swing with a few adjustments. First, open your stance by aligning your feet and shoulders about 25 to 30 degrees left of the target. Position the ball forward, just inside your left heel, and work your feet down into the sand. Next, weaken your grip slightly by turning your hands counterclockwise on the grip. Choke down toward the steel an inch or so, too. Then swing the club with your hips, just like a pitch shot, while keeping your eyes on the spot an inch or so behind the ball where you want to strike the sand, not on the ball itself. The ball should pop out, riding a handful of sand, and land softly. I strongly recommend that you swing slowly and finish the swing.

For a buried lie, square up your stance and the club face, then bring the club down sharply, striking the sand behind the ball. A shallow cut won't work when the ball's buried—you have to chop it out. Also, play for plenty of roll.

For uphill and downhill lies in the sand, the trick is to swing along the contour of the ground. For an uphill lie, place most of your weight on your back foot, so that you're leaning back and your shoulders are parallel with the sand. For a downhill lie, place most of your weight on your front foot. Then simply swing with the slope.

When the ball is below your feet in a bunker, increase your knee flex and aim slightly left of the target. When the ball is above your feet, stand up straight, choke down on the grip and aim slightly to the right of your target.

From wet or hard-packed sand, use your pitching wedge. From powdery sand, open the face of your sand wedge and concentrate on making a shallow cut.

For a sand shot of 30 yards or more, your stance should be slightly open, the club face square and your weight favoring your left side. Then use your normal pitch-shot swing and strike the sand just behind the ball. This may be the toughest shot in golf and it takes practice to play well.

From fairway bunkers where a full swing is involved, you can play either a high "cut" shot or low "punch" shot, depending on the circumstances. For the cut shot, open your stance slightly and position the ball forward about an inch. Also, use one club longer than you would from that distance. Then swing the club outside your normal plane, bringing it down sharply and striking the ball first.

To hit a punch shot from a fairway trap, align your shoulders square to the target line, but your feet and hips should be slightly open. Position the ball back about two inches so your hands will be ahead of the ball at address. Also, take one more club than you normally would with a shot of that distance, and choke down. On the backswing, make only about half a hip turn and a three-quarter shoulder turn. Coming down, strike the ball first and finish with your belt buckle facing the target but with your hands low, about shoulder height.

HARDPAN, ROUGH, AND UNEVEN LIES

Contrary to what a lot of weekend golfers think, hitting a good shot from a hardpan lie isn't hard. By hardpan I mean those flat, dry, sparsely covered areas you can find on almost any golf course. With two simple adjustments to your setup, you can use your normal swing, so there's no reason to be afraid of these shots.

To put this is in its proper perspective, most touring professionals consider a perfect lie to be a tight one, almost like hardpan. It allows them to strike the ball cleanly and put the maximum amount of spin on it for control. Most amateurs, however, prefer grassy lies, because they can get the ball in the air even if they mis-hit it. But lush, grassy lies also spawn fliers— those no-backspin shots that sail long and usually into trouble. Rather than being anxious about hardpan, you should appreciate it for how cleanly you can hit shots from it and how much control you have over the ball's flight.

Here are the two adjustments you need to make.

First, reposition the ball so that it's about an inch farther back in your stance than usual. This will set your hands slightly ahead of the club face at address.

Second, redistribute your weight at address so that slightly more of it is on your left foot. Normally, you should have 60 percent on your left side; to hit a shot from hardpan, favor your left side even more, say 70 percent.

With the ball positioned back an inch and your weight redistributed, you can use your normal swing, because a clean, descending blow with your hands ahead of the club face at impact is ensured. You don't have to change anything else.

Be careful, however. While this technique applies to both woods and irons, I don't recommend hitting a shot from hardpan with a fairway wood unless it's your second shot on a par-5 hole and you have plenty of room for error. Hitting a wood from hardpan is no cinch, even for a good player, so before you pull one out of the bag, consider the consequences of a less than perfect shot. Ask yourself, "Can I still reach the green in regulation if I mis-hit it?" If the answer is no, then I'd recommend laying up with an iron.

Rough

When your ball comes to rest in the long grass, it means you've hit it where you shouldn't have and there may be a price to pay. If the rough is heavy and you've drawn a bad lie, you should forget any thought of heroics and begin thinking in terms of a salvage operation. Perhaps by simply getting the ball back to the fairway you can still make par with a good approach shot and a one-putt. The unpardonable sin under these circumstances is to try something risky and leave your ball in the tall stuff.

Select a lofted club (the sand wedge is usually a good choice), open your stance, swing the club up steeply, then bring it down sharply, almost as if you were dropping the club head on the ball. This is no time to be worried about style points. Your major concern is to get the ball back to the fairway, even if your action looks more like a gouge than a swing.

If the lie permits you to advance the ball some, then consider playing the shot so that your next one will be a full swing with a favorite club. For example, if your pitching wedge is an old friend and you consistently hit it 110 yards, then try to advance your ball to a spot approximately 110 yards from the hole, making your approach shot much easier.

Sometimes, even in heavy rough, you'll draw a good lie—one where you can get the club face on the ball almost cleanly, giving you a realistic chance of getting the ball to the green. There are two ways to play it. You can hit the shot either like a high-trajectory, soft-landing cut or a low-trajectory, hard-running punch.

To hit the former, you open your stance slightly, position the ball forward an inch or two, swing the club up outside as if you were going to hit a fade, then down steeply. I would also recommend that you increase your left-hand grip pressure a little. The ball should pop up quickly and fly high.

By swinging on an upright plane, you lessen the amount of grass that can grab the hosel of your club and shut its face at impact. You also reduce the amount of grass that can get between the club face and the ball. Even though you will get some backspin, you won't get as much as you would from a good lie in the fairway, so allow for some roll. And even though your stance was open, the ball won't curve much left to right either.

The second way to play this shot is to align yourself parallel to the target line, position the ball back in your stance, square the club face, then hit down on the ball sharply. Make sure that your hands stay ahead of the club face through impact. The ball will come out low and hot. Obviously, a punch isn't the shot to play if there's a hazard or obstruction between you and the flag, but it's fine when the green is open in front. It's also good in windy conditions.

On full shots from the rough, I don't advise using long irons. Fairway woods are the better choice, because the contoured shape of their heads allows them to slide through the grass without snagging. The baffy, or 5-wood as it's called today, is particularly well suited for duty in the long grass. It's designed to hit the ball about as far as a 2-iron, but you can choke down on it and use it from shorter distances out of the rough.

Sometimes you'll miss the putting surface with your approach and your ball will end up in heavy greenside rough. If you're lucky and get a good lie, you can play it as a normal chip shot. However, if you have a bad lie, the shot to play is a pitch-shot/sand-shot hybrid.

Use your sand wedge for this one. Open your stance, put most of your weight on your left side, and position the ball just back of where you would play it for a sand shot. You also want the club face open slightly, so weaken your grip a few degrees. Swing the club up abruptly, then hit down *behind* the ball and accelerate through. It's like an explosion shot from grass. The ball should pop up and land softly. It will come out without spin, however, like a knuckleball, so plan on some roll.

Practice will certainly improve your ability to hit this type of shot, but even the best players in the world have trouble getting close to the hole consistently. That's why at the U.S. Open, where the greenside rough is generally awful, you'll hear players shouting for their errant approach shots to get in the bunkers.

From light rough, your biggest concern is hitting a flier. Sometimes you can play it successfully by using a more lofted club; other times, a more lofted club will just leave you short of the green. My advice is to plan your shot so that if it doesn't come off the way you wanted, the ball will end up where your chances of a successful recovery are good.

Uneven Lies

Few amateurs practice hitting shots from sloping terrain, but even a modest grade can have significant effects on the ball's flight. In order to play from uneven lies successfully, you must make a few adjustments.

For uphill and downhill lies, it's important to set up with your spine roughly perpendicular to the ground so that you can swing *with* the slope. To accomplish that for an uphill lie, most of your weight should be on your right foot so that your body is leaning to the right. Position the ball forward in your stance and allow for the ball to curve right to left like a draw. I would also recommend that you use one club more (e.g., instead of a 7-iron, I would select a 6-iron) and choke down half an inch.

For a downhill lie, the procedure is just the opposite. Put most of your weight on your left foot so you're leaning to the left. Position the ball back in your stance and align yourself left

For an uphill lie, put most of your weight on your back foot and position the ball forward.

of the target as if you were playing a fade, because the ball will curve left to right. Also, use one club less (e.g., a 7-iron instead of a 6-iron), because the slope, in effect, de-lofts the shot.

From a sidehill lie where the ball is above your feet, stand up straight and choke down on the club. Position the ball back in your stance, because your swing plane is flatter than normal. The tendency is to hook the ball, so plan for a big right-to-left bend and a lower trajectory.

From a lie where the ball is below your feet, position the ball slightly forward in your stance and flex your knees. It's usually a

For a downhill lie, put most of your weight on your front foot and position the ball back in your stance.

When the ball is above your feet, choke down on the club and aim to the right of your target.

When the ball is below your feet, increase your knee flex and aim to the left of your target.

good idea to take one club more because of the longer shaft and to swing more easily. Take into consideration that the ball should curve left to right like a slice.

Maintaining your balance is important on every swing, but it's crucial when playing shots from sloping terrain. I would strongly recommend that you always rehearse a shot from an uneven lie by taking a practice swing or two.

APPLICATION

"I hit that ball as far as I could swing at it."

As a golfer, I've been very fortunate.

My mother was a Western Kentucky Ladies Champion and I learned to play as a boy. I caddied regularly at the club my parents were members of in Henderson, Kentucky, and the club's professional, Charles Lamb, a transplanted Scot, took time from a busy schedule to teach me. When he left to take another job, his replacement, Del Hamner, worked with me, too, and kept my interest up.

Across the river in Evansville, Indiana, were two other men who were positive influences: Bob Hamilton, winner of the 1944 PGA Championship, and Dutch Rittenhouse. Bob was a great wedge player, and Dutch had wonderful tempo and one of the most stylish swings I've ever seen.

All of these men are gone now, but the time they shared with me and the patience they showed left a lasting impression.

During the Korean Conflict, I joined the Air Force and was stationed in Japan for a time. I had the opportunity to play Kasumigaseki, site of the 1957 World Cup. That was my first experience with a true championship course. I remember at the time that the course record was 69. That's how tough it was. I saw some excellent Japanese players there, too, like Torakichi "Pete" Nakamura and Koichi Ono. What a great swing Nakamura had!

I can remember going to the base library and checking out Sam Snead's book, *How to Play Golf*, and another by Lloyd Mangrum. Both were full of photographs and I would take them to the driving range and try to get myself into the same positions. Then Tommy Armour's book, *How to Play Your Best Golf*

All the Time, came out and I read it over and over. I was amazed at how he had conveyed the swing so succinctly.

Back in the States, I played on some fine Armed Forces teams and my golfing education continued. For example, at our base were players like Mike Krack, Walker Inman, Jr., and Dow Finsterwald. You can learn a lot by watching people of that caliber.

When I got out of the service, I enrolled at the University of Kentucky and played on the team there, but my heart wasn't really in it. Arnold Palmer was coming onto the scene then, and President Eisenhower was an avid golfer. Being a professional was suddenly very glamorous. You got to wear alpaca sweaters with big sleeves and had your name on your bag. Boy, that was for me! So, I turned pro.

In 1960, Sam Snead was the head professional at the Boca Raton Hotel and Royal Palm Yacht and Country Club in Boca Raton, Florida, and I was hired as his resident professional. A recommendation by Bill Campbell had a lot to do with that. Bill liked the way I talked and thought I had a good eye.

Sam wasn't one to talk about his game, but I got lessons just by playing with him. I watched his every move. Sometimes, I would even stand in his footprints on the tee (he never knew it), just to see how my stance compared to his.

It was at Boca Raton that I met Tommy Armour. One of the members was a good friend of his and I asked the member if it would be possible to meet him sometime.

"Sure," he replied. "You're welcome to play with us if you want to. He'll be down Wednesday and we tee off at one o'clock."

I assure you that while I was in Japan, reading Sam's and Tommy's books, the thought never occurred to me that one day I might be in the same room with them, much less get to play golf with them. Now, while working for and getting to play with Sam, I was going to meet and play golf with Tommy Armour.

I will never forget that day. He hadn't said much when we were introduced and I was really nervous on the tee. He was over at the cart fiddling with his clubs while I was looking out of the corner of my eye to see if he was watching me swing. Eventually, I decided I had to hit it whether Tommy was watching me or not. And that's the way it was all day. It seemed like every time I addressed the ball, he was busy doing something.

I shot 70 and we were playing it all the way back, so I was pleased. But that's what Tommy shot, too! I was amazed at how well and how far he could still hit the ball. Keep in mind that he was in his late sixties or early seventies at the time and only had the one good eye.

Afterward, in the locker room, I went up to him, stuck my hand out and said, "Mr. Armour, I really enjoyed that. You've been my idol for years. By any chance, did you see me hit any shots?"

"I saw every shot, laddie," he replied. "You've got a beautiful swing, especially your footwork."

I was stunned. (Since that day, I've never changed my idea of proper footwork and the lower body swing. If you took a lesson from me back then and another today, you would hear the same thing.)

I managed to stammer, "Well, is there anything I should work on?"

"There's a few things. If you'll pick me up Monday morning and take me to Delray Country Club, I'll watch you hit some balls."

And the rest, as they say, is history.

The first thing Tommy required of all his students was that they learn to hit a wedge properly. His contention was (as is mine) that if you can't do that, you've got no business pulling anything else out of the bag. So, that day, I worked very hard with my wedge.

Now, I was a young buck then who regularly posted scores in the 60's and after dozens of balls, I asked him when I could hit a 5-iron or a driver.

"When I'm satisfied with the way you hit the wedge, I'll watch you hit something else," he replied curtly.

And that was the end of that discussion. He was a man of few words and you'd better pay attention when he spoke.

Having been given the opportunity to work with golf's premier teacher, I practiced like I hadn't practiced in a long time. Tommy wanted me to be able to control wedge shots of varying lengths. He thought that the best way to do that for anything less than a full shot was to use a "9 o'clock-to-3 o'clock" swing. In other words, on the backswing, the arms go up to 9 o'clock (visualizing a clock's face), then to 3 o'clock on the follow-through. Distance was controlled by the speed of the lower body's turn.

So, on my driving range, I put up markers at different distances and hit balls to them by the hour. Before long, I became very accurate. Then I progressed to the next stage and learned to hit different types of shots to those markers. I could hit high lobs or low knockdowns by changing the ball's position, and draws or fades by altering my swing plane.

When I became proficient with the wedge, Tommy said, "Now, let me see you hit a 7-iron. It's the same swing, but with a bigger turn."

That's the way he taught. He thought that if you were good, you should be able to hit a 2-iron 200 yards or 100 yards and any distance in between. It's similar to Lee Trevino's philosophy. Lee told me once that he doesn't have just 14 clubs in his bag, he's got about 75 because he can hit each one high or low, bend it left or right, and he can hit each one about any distance he wants to hit it.

In a sense, today's players aren't as fortunate as the players of my day because they don't have the benefit of anything but one shot—high and straight. There are very few of them out there now who can hit a 5-yard cut or draw. Of course, most don't care because they're making so much money with that one shot they can hit. Paul Azinger, however, has had the benefit of what I've learned and, like Trevino, he has about 75 clubs in his bag, too.

After working for Sam, I took a head professional job up the coast in Titusville, Florida, and continued to teach. My friend J. C. Goosie sent dozens of mini-tour players to me for help. And each winter, Moe Norman came down from Canada to keep everybody at my course entertained. I worked with players like Tommy Aaron, Homero Blancas, and Randy Glover, too.

While I was there, I helped a student from nearby Brevard Community College named Mike Smith. In a sense, he was my first real success. He went on to win the NCAA Division II Championship in Flint, Michigan, with a record score. Today, he's a consistent money winner on the PGA Tour. While working with Mike, I realized that what I really wanted to do with my life was to teach young people with more talent than I had how to be better players.

Then, in 1979, Paul Azinger came along.

He was just out of high school and having trouble breaking 80. I had a big driving range then, with all the room in the world, but Paul had a hard time keeping it on the property. There was an airport on one side and a street on the other and, frankly, I was afraid he was going to hit an airplane or a car. But he was such a refreshing young man and so likable that I decided to help him. (It's only partially true, as some people have said, that I did it to keep my insurance rates down.)

I spent a lot of time with him that first year. He went home to Bradenton that summer and really worked on his game, much like I had with Armour. When he came back to school in September, he could play.

He made the team at Brevard, then went on to Florida State and made the team there. He qualified for the PGA Tour on his first try, but lost his card and played the mini-tours for a while. His second time through the Tour Qualifying School, however, he led the pack, and he hasn't looked back. Today, Paul Azinger is one of the best players in the world. I can't tell you how satisfying it is to pick up the newspaper and read where Paul, or any of my other students, has won a tournament or played well.

I've spent a lifetime in golf and my theories have come from studying the greats, playing with them and taking lessons from them. When you're fortunate enough to have people like Bob Hamilton, Sam Snead, Tommy Armour, and Julius Boros as friends, some of what they know has to rub off.

The game has evolved and the best golfers today play a different game than fifty years ago. They're bigger, stronger, and have the benefit of improved equipment and extremely well-maintained courses, so it's no surprise that the scores are better. However, the act itself of striking a golf ball hasn't changed. You still must generate club-head speed and apply it squarely to the ball and, in my opinion, no one has devised a better method for doing that than the one I teach.

Hopefully, in these pages, I've passed on to you some of what a lot of fine players gave to me. I'll leave you with these three stories.

One day while playing with Tommy Armour, I hit a good drive on a par-5 hole that doglegged to the right. I'd put a little fade spin on it, too, so after carrying a fairway bunker at the corner, the ball went right around the dogleg. I'd made a smooth, easy swing and caught it flush, and the shot had come off exactly as I'd pictured it. From there, with a good long iron, I knew I could reach the green in two.

As we walked back to the cart, Tommy told me it was a fine shot and asked me if I'd hit it hard.

"Oh, no," I replied, nonchalantly. "I didn't hit it hard at all. I can hit it farther than that."

He promptly fished a sleeve of new balls out of his bag, handed them to me, and said, "I've got ten dollars that says you can't get one of those by it."

Well, I remember huffing and puffing and hitting those three balls as hard as I could, and I didn't get one of them within fifteen yards of my drive.

After I paid off the bet, he told me, "Whenever you hit a shot the way you hit that drive, don't take the reserve power you didn't feel like you used and put it into the next swing. Always back off a notch and hit the next one easier. If you'd done that just now, you might have been putting my money in your pocket instead of me putting yours in mine."

Playing with Sam Snead one day at Boca Raton, I noticed that on the par-4 holes, we were driving within a few yards of each other, but on the par-5 holes, at least the ones where the fairway was wide, he was always twenty or twenty-five yards ahead of me. After I realized what was happening, I watched him like a hawk, but I still had no idea where the extra distance was coming from. After the round, when we got back to the pro shop, I asked him about it.

"You didn't look like you were swinging any harder, Sam. What's the secret?"

"I wasn't swinging any harder. I was just making a bigger turn."

Well, the next time we played, I knew what to look for. Before, I'd been watching his hands and arms, but this time I kept my eyes on his lower body. Sure enough, he was making a bigger turn with his hips, which allowed him to make a bigger turn with his shoulders without creating tension in his upper body.

From then on, whenever I needed a few extra yards and the fairway was generous, I didn't try to hit the ball harder with my hands and arms, I made a bigger turn with my hips.

In 1963, I played a round of golf with Julius Boros in Ft. Lauderdale. He'd recently won the U.S. Open at Brookline, beating Arnold Palmer and Jackie Cupit in a playoff, and that day he was practicing for the upcoming World Series of Golf.

On one hole, he hit a fabulous 2-iron shot, high and soft, that carried about 225 yards, covering the flag all the way. I'd seen other players hit 2-irons that far, but they'd all looked like they were about to come out of their shoes. Julius, however, had swung with his usual easy tempo, as if he wanted to hit the ball 125 yards instead of 225 yards!

Curious as to just how far he could hit a 2-iron, I asked, "What would happen if you really swung hard at one?"

He shrugged. "I probably wouldn't hit the green."

That surprised me. "What do you mean?"

"John, I hit that ball as far as I could *swing* at it," he said. "If

I went at it harder, then I would be *hitting* at it and I'd lose control. It probably wouldn't go as far, and I'm sure it wouldn't fly as straight."

For a moment, I was back in Henderson, Kentucky, and Mr. Charles Lamb was telling a very young John Redman, "Son, it's like you're swinging a rope and a rock."

Since that day with Julius, I've never tried to hit a ball any farther than I could swing at it.

BIBLIOGRAPHY

Instructional Articles by John Redman

Redman, John, with Robert Carney. "Strong Grip, Strong Turn." *Golf Digest*, August 1987, pp. 52–55.

"An Interview with John Redman." *Golf Illustrated*, March 1988, pp. 37–41.

Redman, John. "The Hips—Turn Level, Turn a Lot." *Golf Illustrated*, August 1988, pp. 25–26.

———. "Hang Loose for a Bigger Turn." *Golf Illustrated*, January/February 1989, pp. 74–75.

———. "The Pause at the Top." *Golf Illustrated*, June 1989, pp. 82–83.

———. "Knock It Down." *Golf Illustrated*, December 1989, pp. 47–49.

———. "Letting Go." *Golf Illustrated*, February, 1990, pp. 57–58.

———. "The Lag." *Golf Illustrated*, May 1990, pp. 42–43.

———. "Hardpan Made Easy." *Golf Illustrated*, August 1990, pp. 25–27.

———. "Chip It Crisp—the One-Club Approach." *Golf Illustrated*, October 1990, pp. 25–27.

———. "Taking a Stand." *Golf Illustrated*, December 1990, pp. 39–40.

———. "Hitting the Draw." *Golf Illustrated,* May 1991, pp. 25–27.

———. "Where to Play It—Ball Position Is Everything." *Golf Illustrated,* July 1991, pp. 47–49.

———, with T. J. Tomasi. "Narrow Your Stance to Widen Your Arc." *Golf Illustrated,* March 1992, pp. 86–87.

———, with T. J. Tomasi. " 'X' Marks the Spot—Improve Your Knee Action, Improve Your Game." *Golf Illustrated,* April 1992, pp. 60–61.

Recommended Reading

Armour, Tommy. *How to Play Your Best Golf All the Time.* New York: Simon & Schuster, 1953.

Boomer, Percy. *On Learning Golf.* New York: Knopf, 1946.

Jones, Ernest, and David Eisenberg. *Swing the Clubhead.* New York: Dodd, Mead, 1952.

Jones, Robert Tyre, Jr. *Bobby Jones on Golf.* New York: Doubleday, 1966.

———. *Bobby Jones on the Basic Golf Swing.* New York: Doubleday, 1969.

———. *Golf Is My Game.* New York: Doubleday, 1960.

Millman, Dan. *Way of the Peaceful Warrior.* Tiburon, Calif.: H. J. Kramer, 1984.

Murphy, Michael. *Golf in the Kingdom.* New York: Viking, 1972.

Snead, Sam. *How to Play Golf.* Garden City, N.Y.: Garden City Books, 1946.